# Growing Herbs

# Growing Herbs

## John Mason

Meyerbooks, *Publisher*
Glenwood, Illinois

**Acknowledgements**

Text written and complied by John Mason.
Editorial assistants: Iain Harrison, Paul Plant and
other staff from the Australian Horticultural
Correspondence School.
Contributions from the Australian Horticultural
Correspondence School and staff at the Bread
Research Institute, North Ryde, Sydney.
Photographs: John Mason and Leonie Mason.
Illustrations: John Mason and Hans Manson.

**Library of Congress Cataloging-in-Publication Data**

Mason, John.
  Growing herbs / John Mason.
     p.   cm.
  Originally published: Kenthurst, Australia: Kangaroo Press, 1993.
  Includes index.
  ISBN 0-916638-50-2
  1. Herb gardening. 2. Herbs. 3. Herbs—Utilization. I. Title.
  SB351.H5M32  1994
  635'.7—dc20                            93-42021
                                                 CIP

ISBN 0-916638-50-2

# Contents

# 1 Growing Herbs

## What is a herb?

The scientific definition of a herb is *a plant which has no persistent stem above the ground* (i.e. the leaves and stems die back to the roots after a period of growth). By this definition, strictly speaking you would call ornamental plants such as daffodils and dahlias herbs, as well as 'useful' plants such as mint and garlic.

The more popular definition of a herb is *any plant whose roots, bark, stems, leaves, seeds or flowers are used for culinary, medicinal or perfumery purposes.*

Herbs are essentially plants which are grown because of the characteristics derived from the oils or other chemical components found in their tissue. They come in all shapes and sizes: from bulbs and herbaceous perennials to woody trees and shrubs. Many are scented plants; all provide something which is useful, for example, in cooking, cosmetics, craft, pest control or natural therapies.

## What's so great about herbs?

Many of the more popular herbs are among the easiest and hardiest plants to grow in the garden. They are fast-growing, there is generally little cost involved in growing them, and they have an extremely diverse range of uses. These factors, coupled with a growing preference for natural alternatives, have resulted in a revival of interest in the use of herbs.

Herbs are often grown by themselves in a special 'herb garden', although there is no real reason why they can't be mixed in with other plants throughout the garden. Many people grow herbs in tubs, hanging baskets or pots, placed on patios, in window boxes or even indoors. Whichever way you choose, growing herbs will add a new and exciting dimension to your garden. Even old hands at herb gardening continue to be amazed by the diversity of herb varieties and their uses.

Herbs have been gathered, grown and used in all parts of the world for thousands of years. The ancient Greeks, Egyptians and Romans all used herbs, as did most other early civilizations throughout the world. Most of the herbs which we commonly use today were developed by European herbalists, particularly through the Middle Ages and the Renaissance. Many medicinal properties of herbs have been thoroughly tested over the centuries and their credibility has been firmly established

In recent years there has been considerable interest by scientists and enthusiastic amateurs in determining the effects of herb usage and the components of the herbs which cause these effects. Much effort is also being spent on introducing new herbs into widespread cultivation, including traditional herbs used by indigenous peoples. This suggests that the use of herbs has a strong and exciting future.

With a history which spans thousands of years, it

is no wonder the difference between fact and fiction has often become blurred with regard to herbs. Herbs have long been associated, in many different cultures, with things magical or supernatural, perhaps due to the miraculous healing powers of some herbs. In truth, despite the fact that there has been a great deal written or said about many herbs which is totally wrong, there has also been just as much written or said which is correct.

Today's herb user has a challenge to identify what is right and what is wrong. When reading about herbs, you should look at the background of the author to determine how authorative their material is and you should cross-reference information on herbs with as many sources as possible. You could also look in-depth at the history of that herb.

# Buying your plants

Herbs can be purchased in 5 cm tubes or larger pots. Most herbs grow so fast that tubestock is generally the most economical means of purchase. Larger pots are usually better for the slower growing woody herbs such as rosemary, lavender and bay tree.

When purchasing your plants you should look for the following features as an indication of the plant's health:

Foliage—Do the leaves look healthy or are they mottled or discoloured?
Root tips—Are they discoloured? Do they appear to be circling around the base of the pot?
Growing tips—Are they lush and healthy-looking?
Stems—Are the stems vigorous?

It is very important to remember that if you want healthy herbs in your house or garden then you should only purchase good quality plants. Don't compromise—buying good quality plants works out cheaper in the long run!

# Propagation

Most herbs are easy to propagate. Seed is the easiest and commonest method of propagation. However, it is often preferable to start your plants from cuttings or division because these methods allow you to produce plants which have identical characteristics to the parent plants.

## Seed Propagation

To propagate plants by seed, first consider the health and freshness of the seed, the correct season for sowing, and the recommended sowing procedures.

### The Basic Steps
1. Use equipment that is clean and free from infectious diseases. If you are reusing old equipment (trays or pots), sterilise them with household bleach (diluted to 1 or 2%).
2. Sow seeds in a tray or pot filled to just below the rim with good quality seed-raising mixture. The mix should be lightly moistened and allowed to drain freely before the seeds are sown.

Use a dibble (a small pointed stick) to make small holes just deep and big enough for large single seeds or make a shallow furrow and sow seeds in single lines. Smaller seeds can be spread evenly over the mix. The seeds should not be sitting too close to each other, otherwise disease may be increased and separation of the seedlings may be difficult.
3. Cover seeds with a fine layer of seed-raising mixture to improve germination. As a general rule, seeds are covered to about twice their diameter (alternatively, you could have made the holes and depressions this depth originally). Gently apply pressure to improve the seed/mix contact—this will speed up germination. Gently water in.
4. Position the seed tray or pot in a sheltered position where it will receive some light but not full sun. Deep shade should be avoided. A greenhouse or cold frame is often used, particularly in cooler climates.

Ensure that the seed tray or pot is kept moist but not wet. As seedlings appear, continue watering and rotate the pot or tray if the seedlings are bending due to inadequate light (even better—move plants to a sunnier position).
5. As the seedlings continue to grow, applications of weak soluble fertiliser will assist plant development. When they are past the two-leaf stage (i.e. when more leaves start to develop) you can transplant the seedlings into individual pots or directly into the ground (depending on the variety).

At all times you will need to provide adequate

moisture to promote growth and to minimise shock during the transplanting process.

## Cutting Propagation

Cuttings can be classified two different ways:

1. According to the time of year and the stage of growth of the parent plant.
• Softwood cuttings are taken in spring when the young growth on the plant is soft.
• Hardwood cuttings are taken in winter when the previous season's growth has hardened. Common hardwood cuttings include tip growth taken from conifers and sections of stem taken from deciduous plants.
• Semi-hardwood cuttings are usually taken in late summer or early autumn when recent spring growth is in the process of hardening.

2. According to the part of the plant which is used.
• **Stem cutting** A section of stem, usually (but not always) with some leaves left on the top. The lower

Many herbs can be grown easily by cuttings. As with most varieties, these scented geranium cuttings are prepared for planting by taking pieces of healthy stems around 5 to 7 cm long, then removing most of the lower leaves.
When planted into a sandy potting mix they will produce roots and develop into a new plant.

leaves are always removed. There should be a node (the point at which a bud emerges) at the bottom of the cutting and another node at the top of the cutting. There may be one or several nodes in between (depending on the plant and the size of the cutting).
• **Tip cutting** A stem cutting taken from the growing tip of a plant.

• **Heel cutting** A stem cutting of 1-year-old wood with a small section of 2-year-old wood attached to the base. The cutting is normally prepared by tearing side-shoots from a small branch or stem. The torn section is then neatly trimmed with a knife or pair of secateurs.
• **Nodal cutting** A stem cutting without a heel. The base of the cutting is made with a right angle cut, just below a node (i.e. where a leaf joins the stem).
• **Basal cutting** A stem cutting with the base of the cutting taken at the point where the young shoot joins the older branch. At this point there is often some swelling in the stem. Unlike the heel cutting, the basal cutting does not necessarily contain any older wood.
• **Leaf bud cutting** A cutting using a full leaf (i.e. leaf blade and stalk) attached to a small piece of the stem. The bud at the junction of the leaf and stem is retained.
• **Leaf cutting** Either a section of a leaf or a full leaf including the leaf stalk (i.e. petiole). In the case of a section of a leaf being used, the cutting must include part of a major leaf vein.
• **Cane cutting** A small section of cane containing only one or two nodes and no leaves. The cutting is inserted horizontally with an upward-facing bud showing above the surface of the media. Heating and misting are essential for success.
• **Root cutting** A section of young (1–3-year-old) roots, 2–10 cm long, preferably from young plants. Cuttings are planted horizontally, 2–4 cm deep.
• **Bulb cuttings** A mature bulb cut vertically into 8 or 10 sections, with each section containing part of the basal plate. Each of these sections can be further divided by cutting down between the scales. Plant vertically with just the tips of the cut sections showing.

Most herb cuttings are taken from stems in late summer or autumn. Depending on the herb, the cuttings are 3 to 8 cm long. The lower cut is made just below a node (i.e. where the leaf is joined to the stem). The upper cut is made just above a node, except in tip cuttings where the growth tip is often retained.

The bottom two-thirds of the leaves should be cut off with a sharp tool—do not tear the leaves! Several cuttings can be inserted into a pot containing 25% peat moss and 75% coarse washed sand (i.e. propagating or aquarium sand). Gently firm the mix around the cuttings and keep well-watered until the first roots grow out of the holes at the bottom of the pot. At this stage, carefully remove the cuttings, making sure not to damage the roots and transplant each one into individual pots filled with loose, well-drained and clean potting mix.

## Division/Separation

Division involves separating the plant clump into individual small groups which can be replanted to grow on. Many creeping or clump-forming herbs (e.g. chives, thymes, mints, etc.) can be divided to form new plants.

Many creeping or suckering types of herbs like this peppermint can simply be taken out of a pot (or dug up) and cut or gently pulled apart to create new plants.

The process involves lifting the plant out of the ground and removing excessive foliage and roots; dividing the plant clump with the use of two garden forks, a knife or secateurs; and then replanting the separated clumps.

Bulbs are simply lifted after the foliage has died down and separated by hand.

## Layering

Simple layering involves bringing a piece of plant stem down to the ground and burying it while still attached to the parent plant. The surface of the stem should be lightly cut or abraded to improve root development and establishment. It is optional to apply rooting hormone to the abraded surface. Rocks, tent pegs, or pegs made from thick bent wire, are ideal for holding stems down. Over time, roots will grow from the damaged or cut bark. The plant can then be severed from the parent plant.

Air layering is done above the ground. A branch is chosen and the bark removed for a width of up to 2 cm. Alternatively, three-quarters of the bark is removed in this area so that some nutrients may still travel up and down the stem. Once again, an application of rooting hormone is optional. The area is then covered with a moist layer of spaghnum or peat moss and firmly sealed with plastic. In time, roots will develop and the upper part of the air layer can be cut off and potted up or planted in the ground.

# Soils and potting mixes

A major factor in successfully growing any plant, including herbs, is the media in which they grow. Some plants grow successfully in water, on trees or rocks; however the majority of plants are grown in soil or a substitute that supplies similar properties such as a soilless potting mix.

## What is soil?

Soil provides the plant with physical support, nutrients, air and water. It is composed of five main ingredients:

1. Mineral particles such as sand, silt and clay.
2. Organic materials such as dead and decaying plants, animals and animal products.
3. Air which is found in the voids between soil particles.
4. Water which usually contains dissolved plant nutrients and other elements.
5. Living organisms such as earthworms, viruses, nematodes, bacteria, etc.

Different combinations of these ingredients will produce different types of soils, each with its own set of properties. A good soil will:

- Provide adequate drainage.
- Have good aeration (i.e. contain plenty of air in the soil).
- Retain adequate moisture to sustain healthy plant growth.
- Provide adequate support for the plants.
- Be free of harmful pests and diseases or pollutants.
- Have the correct pH for the plants (i.e. not too acidic or alkaline).
- Have adequate nutrients to support healthy growth.

Potting mixes should also have these properties. Many potting mixes are soil-free with materials such as pine bark, sawdust, perlite, rice hulls and wood chips being substituted in place of the mineral components found in soils. Soilless mixes can be an excellent media for growing plants as they are generally free of the disease organisms that live in soils.

## Soil structure

Soil structure refers to the arrangement of the mineral particles in the soil. Good soil structure means that the various mineral particles are bound together in crumbs of varying sizes, creating spaces (known as pore spaces) of varying sizes between the crumbs. Soils with poor structure have few crumbs and pore spaces, and may appear as a fine powder or large clods. If a soil has good structure, then it will have good drainage and aeration.

## Improving soils

Most soils can be improved. In particular, nearly all soils can be improved by adding organic matter such as well-rotted compost, sawdust and manure directly into the soil, or by using them as surface mulches.

Heavy soils with poor drainage and aeration can be improved by the addition of coarse material such as sand and organic matter. Soils that drain too readily can be improved by the addition of moisture-retaining materials such as well-rotted compost.

Compacted or poorly structured soils can be improved by the incorporation of coarse material, organic matter and a dressing of lime. Compacted clay soils will also benefit from the addition of gypsum or a commercial soil conditioner such as Maxicrop's 'Clay Breaker'.

## Preparing the soil

All but a few herbs prefer a well-drained but moist soil. Clay soils should have lots of well-rotted compost or manure dug or rotary-hoed into the soil. If the garden is low-lying or poorly drained, you will need to form the soil into mounds or raised beds (bringing in extra soil if necessary). Alternatively, you will need to provide some other form of drainage such as 'agi' pipes.

Very sandy soils also need compost or manure mixed into the soil to improve their ability to hold water. In hot climates, a surface mulch around the herbs will keep the roots cool and reduce water being lost from the soil. A good thick organic mulch will also help control weeds which can be a problem for some weaker-growing herbs.

## Soil pH

This is a measure of the soil's acidity. The soil's pH is measured on a scale of 1 to 14. The neutral point is 7, below 7 is acid and above 7 is alkaline. The majority of plants prefer a pH of around 6 to 7, although most herbs prefer neutral to slightly alkaline soils. Simple pH kits can readily determine the soil's level of acidity or alkalinity.

In acid soils calcium carbonate (lime) may be required to increase the soil pH. About $1/2$–1 kg of lime per square metre is needed on soils with a pH level of 6.0; a double amount is required for a pH level of 5.0. Quantities should be reduced for sandy soils and increased for clay soils.

In very alkaline soils and for those herbs that do prefer acid conditions, the addition of an acidic fertiliser such as sulphate of ammonia will prove beneficial.

Although most herbs are very adaptable to a wide range of soil types, the following herbs are particularly suited to the soil types listed below:

**Alkaline soils**
Catnip, hyssop, juniper, lavender, marjoram, rosemary, salad burnet, summer savory.
**Sandy soils**
Anise, borage, chamomile (Roman), coriander, cumin, evening primrose, fennel, lavender, marjoram, tarragon, thyme, winter savory.
**Loam soils**
Basil, bay, betony, caraway, catnip, chervil, chives,

coriander, dill, fennel, lovage, parsley, rosemary, rue, sage, scented geraniums, tansy, thyme.
**Clay soils**
Bergamot, comfrey, mint, wormwood.

# Composting

All organic material eventually rots down due to the action of micro-organisms. Composting is simply a fast way to harness or control this process.

A ready source of well-rotted organic matter can be obtained by composting waste organic materials such as lawn clippings, household waste, animal manures, sawdust, leaf mould and plant clippings.

Composting will be most rapid when the moisture content of the material is between 40 and 60%—ideally around 50–55%. If you squeeze your composting material it should have about as much moisture as a squeezed-out sponge. Temperatures should be in the range of 40–60° C—ideally around 50° C. To achieve this level, and to provide good aeration, the heap should be turned over and mixed every 2–3 weeks. Under the right conditions the compost will be ready in about 12 weeks.

## What to use in compost?

The best type of compost will result from using the best type of organic material, which should have a ratio of carbon to nitrogen averaging between 25 and 30.

| Organic material | C:N Ratio |
| --- | --- |
| Sawdust (fresh) | 500 : 1 |
| Sawdust (old) | 200 : 1 |
| Composted pine bark (average) | 200 : 1 |
| Paper | 170 : 1 |
| Straw (wheat) | 128 : 1 |
| Straw (general) | 100 : 1 |
| Straw (oat) | 48 : 1 |
| Corn stalks, leaves and cobs | 50 to 100 : 1 |
| Oak leaves | 50 : 1 |
| Bracken leaves | 48 : 1 |
| Green rye grass | 36 : 1 |
| Ash leaves | 30 : 1 |
| Weeds | 30 : 1 |
| Clover (old plants) | 20 to 30 : 1 |

| Organic material | C:N Ratio |
| --- | --- |
| Vegetable peelings | 20 to 30 : 1 |
| Fruit wastes | 35 : 1 |
| Well-rotted manure (average) | 20 : 1 |
| Seaweed (average) | 20 : 1 |
| Pea or bean plants | 15 : 1 |
| Clover (young seedlings) | 12 : 1 |
| Cabbage heads | 12 : 1 |
| Tomato leaves and stems | 12 : 1 |
| Lawn clippings | 12 to 25 : 1 |
| Cow manure (not composted) | 12 : 1 |
| Mature compost | 10 : 1 |
| Comfrey leaves | 10 : 1 |
| Chicken litter (average-with sawdust) | 10 : 1 |
| Chicken manure (no sawdust) | 7 : 1 |
| Blood meal | 4 : 1 |

Materials with a high C/N ratio can be mixed with materials having a low C/N ratio to achieve the desired ratio.

Despite the benefits of using material with the ideal ratio, you can use absolutely anything organic on your compost heap if you wish. Just realize that if the carbon/nitrogen ratios are not right, it may take a very long time for decomposition to occur.

## What can go wrong with compost?

The main reasons for the composting process going too slow are:

1. The compost is too wet.
Foul odours indicate that the heap is too wet. Extra turning or adding dry materials can overcome this problem.

2. The compost is too dry.
If the centre of the heap is dusty, it is far too dry. Simply turn the heap and add water.

3. Lack of nutrients.
Insufficient levels of phosphorus and potassium can reduce the rate of decomposition. Add organic materials with high levels of phosphorus and potassium to rectify this problem.

4. Carbon/nitrogen ratio is incorrect.
Lack of nitrogen because of too much high carbon ratio material is common. Adding organic material with a low carbon nitrogen ratio such as manures or lawn clippings, or nitrogenous fertiliser will help correct this problem.

# Organic gardening and herbs

Organic gardening is a philosophy which involves working with nature rather than against it. It uses methods such as composting, mulching and applying animal and green manures to build and maintain the organic soil matter and increase the population of beneficial soil micro-organisms. It takes advantage of natural predators and uses companion planting and other non-chemical means to control pests and diseases.

In practical terms, organic gardening means following a number of specific gardening practices:

• Plants are grown without the use of artificial chemicals. Fertilisers, pesticides and weedicides are derived from organic materials or other natural materials such as rock dusts. Herb plants are the most common source of natural pesticides.
• Soil fertility and structure is maintained and improved by the continued addition of humus, that is, rotted organic material such as manures and plant material. All organic matter should be from sources free of contamination by artificial chemicals.
• Beneficial insects and other small organisms are encouraged in the garden. Insects which feed off pest species can be introduced as biological control agents, and earthworms and mycorrhizas can be used to improve soil fertility. There are many herbs that attract beneficial organisms to your garden and repel harmful organisms.
• Non-chemical cultural methods are used. For example, physical barriers and traps are used to control pests; crop rotations prevent depletion of soil nutrients and reduce the likelihood of pest or disease problems building up; weeds can be controlled mechanically or by hand.

## Organic Fertilisers

All materials added to composts or used directly on the garden as fertilisers should be free of chemical contamination. This includes antibiotics, growth promotants, etc. that may have been fed to livestock.

### Animal manure

All animal manures are a valuable source of nutrients, either mixed into a compost heap or applied directly on the garden beds.

It is important to have some idea of the nitrogen content of manures because high levels of nitrogen can burn the plant roots. Well-rotted cow, sheep, horse and goat manures are generally safe to use directly on the soil. Pulverised and partly composted cow manure can be used on beds which are to be planted with seedlings on the same day, provided the manure is thoroughly mixed in the top 6–8 cm of soil. (The same treatment with an equal amount of poultry or pigeon manure would be disastrous, with most, if not all of the seedlings dying within a few days.)

### Poulty manure

Poultry manure can be obtained either as pure manure or as dry deep-litter material (i.e. the manure is mixed with woodshavings or straw).

When using pure poultry manure make sure that the chicken farmers have not sprayed the manure heaps with insecticides—this is a common practice in some farms. Deep-litter poultry manure is always a safer bet because it is far less likely to have been sprayed (the chickens eat insects as they scratch through the litter).

### Blood and bone meal

Dried blood, used in a number of commercial organic manures, probably has the highest nitrogen content of any organic manure—about 11.5%. It is, however, expensive. Blood meal contains approximately 1% phosphorus; bone meal contains around 4% nitrogen and over 20% phosphorus.

### Rock dusts

Rock dusts are simply ground-up or crushed rocks. Natural weathering gradually leaches out many of the original nutrient reserves in the soil. Since many of these nutrients originally came from silt or weathered rock, some organic gardeners argue that applying rock dust replenishes the nutrients. Some experts, however, are sceptical about the benefits of rock dusts. Some rock dusts used in gardening are:

Gypsum to supply calcium and sulphur.
Dolomite to supply calcium and magnesium.
Limestone to supply calcium.
Scoria to supply iron.
Basalt to supply calcium, magnesium, phosphorus, potassium and a range of minor nutrients.

## Seaweed

Unlike other plants, many types of seaweed do not contain cellulose. This causes them to rot down faster, making it an ideal material to use in the compost heap.

Seaweed is a rich source of boron, iodine, calcium, magnesium, sodium and other trace elements. Different types of seaweed have different nutrient values. The kelps are the best source of potash (these are the large flat, brown strap-like seaweeds).

Wash harmful surface salt off the plants before use (i.e. leave out in the rain for a while, or soak for an hour or so in a 200-litre drum or trough of water).

It is safe to mulch the garden with a generous layer of seaweed about once every four years. Overuse can lead to nutrient toxicities and cause leaf burn.

### Liquid seaweeds

There are several seaweed liquid fertilisers on the market in Australia, but they do vary in quality. Maxicrop and Seasol are two tried and proven products.

Although seaweed doesn't have high levels of nitrogen, phosphorus or potassium, it does contain a broad spectrum of micronutrients, and many people attest to their plants having strong growth and good health when they use seaweed extracts.

It is difficult to overdose plants with liquid seaweed. In addition to general garden use, seaweed is excellent for promoting growth on newly planted seedlings and indoor plants. Some people even dip cuttings in the solution to encourage root formation.

## Home-made Liquid Manures

Fifty years ago, successful gardeners relied heavily on the frequent use of natural liquid manure supplements. Bags of various animal manures (mostly cow or poultry) were immersed in large wooden barrels filled with water for varying periods before being used to fertilise plants in a diluted form.

Any type of manure is suitable as an infusion. Cow manure (in broken pats) contained in a polynet onion bag and suspended in a large plastic garbage tin of water makes a gentle liquid manure. The bag should be packed full and gently dunked up and down a few times during the brewing period. At the end of three weeks the liquid may be used to fertilise plants in the garden. It is safe to use on young seedlings, but should be diluted by nine parts water to one part liquid manure.

The golden rules in using any liquid manures are 'diluted' and 'frequent'. Strong organic manure can be as disastrous as chemical manures if used injudiciously. Urine is an excellent liquid manure if diluted about 1:20.

## Natural plant foods

The following table gives an indication of the benefits that may be obtained from different materials used as fertilisers or mulches. The figures are averages.

| | Nitrogen (%) | Phosphorus (%) | Potassium (%) |
|---|---|---|---|
| Dried blood meal | 9 to 13 | 1 to 3 | 1 |
| Sewage (fresh) | 5 | 3 | |
| Sewage (digested) | 2 | | |
| Manure (fresh) | 2 | 1 | 1 |
| Manure (dried) | 1 to 2 | 1 to 2 | 3 |
| Bone meal (raw) | 3 | 23 | |
| Bone meal (steamed) | 2 | 30 | |
| Feathers | 3 to 10 | 0.2 | 0.5 |
| Hoof and horn | 7 to 13 | 0.8 | |
| Fish meal | 8 | 8 | |
| Grass clippings | 1 to 3 | 2 | |
| Raw sugar waste | | 8 | |
| Wood ash (average) | | 1 to 2 | 8 |
| Seaweed | 3 | 0.2 | 3 |
| Wheat straw | 0.4 | 0.2 | 1 |
| Oat straw | 0.4 | 0.3 | 1 |
| Barley straw | 0.3 | 0.2 | 0.5 |
| Hay (average) | 1.2 | 0.4 | 1.6 |
| Green bracken leaves | 1.5 | 0.2 | 1.5 |
| Apple cores | 0.5 | 0.02 | 0.1 |
| Coffee grounds (dried) | 2 | 0.4 | 0.7 |
| Citrus peel | 0.2 | 0.1 | 0.2 |
| Peanut shells | 0.8 | 0.15 | 0.5 |
| Tea leaves | 4.2 | 0.6 | 0.4 |

References: *Fertility Gardening* by Hills (1981), publisher David & Charles.
*Hydro Story* by Sherman & Brenizer, publisher Nolo Press.

## Other Organic Materials

The following materials are commonly used in organic gardening. They may be used one or more of the following ways:
• Added to a compost heap.

- Spread on the soil surface as a mulch.
- Dug into the soil to improve soil structure and fertility.

## Ash

Wood ash from a fireplace, stove or open bonfire is a very good source of potash. It can be added to compost heaps (in thin layers) or spread at the base of plants as a potash fertiliser. Potash is easily leached—if the compost remains saturated for several weeks the potash will wash away.

Incinerator ash or burned charcoal is usually not as useful as pure wood ash. Do not use ash which may contain residues from burnt plastics, etc. Briquette or coal ash is not suitable for composting or adding to soil.

Wood ash can also be used as a physical barrier to crawling pests, e.g. snails, slugs, caterpillars and millipedes.

## Hay

There are many different types of hay available, although they vary in their nutrition content. Lucerne hay has a much higher level of nitrogen than grass hay and can be used when relatively fresh. If fresh grass hay is used on the garden, add nitrogen fertiliser (e.g. blood and bone or manure) to the base of each plant.

Avoid using hay or straw which has seed mixed in with it. The seeds may germinate and create a weed problem.

## Leaves

Most leaf litter is ideal as a mulch, but should not make up more than 20% of a compost heap. Large leaves decompose more slowly than smaller leaves and will decompose faster if put through a shredder.

Some leaves, including pine needles and eucalypt leaves, contain toxic chemicals and are not suitable around some types of plants, particularly in cold areas.

Oak or beech leaves are ideal to mulch around acid-loving plants such as blueberries, azaleas and rhododendrons.

## Peat moss

Peat moss is excellent for improving the soil's water-holding ability, both in the garden and in potting and propagating mixes. It is very acidic, so you may need to add lime to compensate. It is also very expensive.

## Prunings

Light prunings can be used as a surface mulch, however they are are best shredded before added to the compost heap. Ideally shredding is done with a mulching machine. Alternatively, finer material can be spread on the ground and shredded by running a lawn mower over the top.

Be careful with easy-to-root plant material—some prunings may take root if left lying around in moist conditions.

## Rubbish

Most household rubbish can be used in an organic garden, either added to a compost heap or used as a mulch. There are some exceptions though!
- Synthetic fibres (e.g. nylon) do not decompose and should be avoided.
- Fats and oils do not decompose readily, and can put a coating over other organic materials, slowing down their rate of decomposition. Fats also tend to attract flies and other pests.
- Plastics—some plastics do not decompose, others will take a long time to break down. In addition, the breakdown products may result in undesirable chemical residues.

## Sawdust

Sawdust can be used as a mulch or dug into the top-soil. A 2–3 cm layer of sawdust is adequate in most situations. However, the rapid rate of decomposition results in nitrogen being 'stolen' from the soil and surrounding plants will need extra feeding.

Fresh sawdust will last as a mulch for several seasons. Old sawdust will rot down and largely disappear in one season. Hardwood sawdusts (e.g. jarrah, red gum and red box) will break down much slower than softwood sawdusts (e.g. pine).

The sawdust should be thoroughly saturated when first delivered to prevent it being blown away by strong winds. It will also need to be kept moist after it is spread on the garden because dried layers tend to form an impermeable crust, preventing water reaching the soil beneath.

## Shavings

Wood shavings can be placed in a 10–12 cm layer on garden beds. Again, you will need to place nitrogenous fertiliser at the base of each plant to compensate for nitrogen lost from the soil to decomposing bacteria.

Wood shavings are light-weight and easy to move about (use a large plastic bag for easy moving). Like sawdust, the shavings will need to be wet down to prevent them being blown away.

### Weeds

The trouble with weeds is that if you use them as a mulch or in compost, they may regrow in the garden and create a serious problem.

This can be avoided by:

• Proper composting. The heat generated in the middle of a compost heap will kill most weeds and their seeds.
• Not using weeds with ripe seeds. If you cut the top off a weed before it produces seed, it is unlikely to regrow.
• Not using perennial weeds. Serious perennial weeds such as blackberry or prickly pear will regrow from even the smallest piece.

### Other materials

Other materials that have been successfully used include feathers, shell grit, rice hulls, poppy straw, waste from seafood processing and cotton meal.

### Worms

The addition of specially bred compost worms achieves a double benefit. Firstly, the action of the worms burrowing through the soil aerates the soil and improves drainage and plant growth. Secondly, the worm castings contain broken-down nutrients which are available to plants in a form similar to liquid fertilisers.

### Mulching

Organic mulches provide several benefits to the garden:

1. The soil remains moist for longer periods.
2. Weed growth is reduced as the mulch smothers existing weeds and prevents new weeds germinating.
3. Plant roots are insulated from extreme heat and cold. Mulch insulates and raises the temperature slightly around the plant through heat generated by decomposing bacteria.
4. Soil nutrition and structure is improved as the mulch decomposes.
5. Soil erosion is reduced.

A variety of substances may be used as mulches, including wood shavings, bark, shredded newspaper, coconut fibre, grass clippings, straw and compost. Mulched plants may need extra fertiliser to offset the nutrients being lost to decomposing bacteria.

Red Tiger Worms are one of several 'super worms' available from worm farms. For the organic gardener, adding these worms to the soil will rapidly improve the fertility and structure of the soil.

# How to Make a No-dig Herb Garden

1. Select a site which receives maximum sunlight.
2. Remove as many weeds as possible.
3. Cover the soil with a layer of newspaper (20–40 sheets thick).
4. Cover the newspaper with a 10–15 cm layer of organic material such as straw, wood shavings or hay. Make sure the hay or straw is free of grass or weed seeds.
5. Next spread a thin (2–4 cm) layer of well-rotted animal manure.
6. Spread 4 cm layer of lucerne hay over the surface.
7. Finish with a layer of organic compost. Make sure the compost has an open texture and is free of weed seeds.
8. Herb seeds can be directly sown into the top layer of compost. The heat generated by the decomposing layers aids seed germination and root growth of new plants.

Building a no-dig garden:
1. Gather materials and remove weeds and grass.

2. Cover the ground surface with thick layers of newspapers.

3. Place alternate layers of straw, compost and manure over the newspaper. Thoroughly wet the layers before planting seedlings.

9. Water the seedlings with an appropriate fertiliser.

You now have a very low maintenance herb garden!

# Feeding Herbs

Most herbs grow rapidly and respond to regular feeding during the growing season. There are three main types of plant foods:

1. Slow release fertilisers: These have a store of concentrated nutrients which are gradually released over a period of weeks or months. The rate of release usually depends on moisture and temperature. In wet and warm conditions, the fertiliser is released into the soil very quickly. In milder, drier weather nutrient release will be slower and the fertiliser will last longer.

2. Quick-acting fertilisers: These dissolve readily in water and the nutrients are immediately available to the plant. They give quick results but can be easily washed away by water moving through the soil.

3. Fertiliser/tonics: These contain the more obscure elements that promote plant growth. They usually contain minor nutrients (which are only needed in tiny quantities, but if they are missing in the soil plant growth can be seriously affected). These fertilisers often also contain plant hormones which stimulate plant growth. This type of fertiliser will help sustain a balanced chemical regime in the soil.

# Planting herbs

There are various ways to plant herbs. This is just one method:

1. Dig a hole one and a half times the depth of the plant's root ball.
2. Place a small amount of fertiliser in the bottom of the hole.
3. Replace one-third of the soil and mix with the fertiliser.
4. Remove the plant from the pot and loosen the roots.
5. Place the plant in the hole and fill in around it with soil.
6. Water in a volume of water equivalent to the size of the hole you dug.
7. Place mulch around the base of the plant and if required tie the plant to a stake.

# Watering herbs

In hot weather the soil needs to be kept moist but not wet. Scratch down to a depth of 2.5 cm—if the soil is dry then the herb should be watered. At the height of the growing season herbs may need to be watered every day.

Potted herbs can be stood in a bowl of water until the soil surface is damp. Never allow the plants to dry out completely or the plants will be damaged when you water them. Herbs in hanging baskets can be watered with a fine aerosol spray in hot weather. Once a week take the basket down to give it a thorough soaking and allow it to drain before rehanging.

## Protecting newly-planted herbs

Often young herb plants need protection when first planted. Planting out seedlings in the open ground is best done in the late afternoon. Never plant in the middle of a hot day. Immediately after planting, water the plant in, ensuring the root zone is thoroughly wet, and then sprinkle a light organic mulch (e.g. compost) around the base to help minimise water loss from the soil. Watering should be frequent and light—perhaps twice daily—until plants begin to grow.

Many herbs are susceptible to damage by wind, sun and frost. These problems can be overcome in the following ways:
• Protect against wind by staking, using tree guards, windbreaks or planting in a protected position, e.g. close to a fence or wall.
• Protect against hot sun by mulching, using tree guards, planting where there will be shade in the hottest part of the day, planting near water or in a cool part of the garden.
• Protect from frost with plastic tree guards, by mulching or planting near a fence, wall or large tree.

## Safe Pest and Disease Control

Most herbs are relatively free of pest and disease problems. The strong oils in their foliage are distasteful to many insects and many herbs contain chemicals with antiseptic properties which kill bacteria and fungal diseases. However some herb plants are prone to a particular disease or pest, for example, rust attacks mint, and greenfly infests parsley during dry weather. In the humid tropics and sub-tropics, cooler climate herbs are often susceptible to disease. Plants with woolly or hairy surface or dense foliage are also more likely to succumb to diseases. Keeping plants well spaced so air can move around them will help reduce humidity and the chance of infection.

A regular check will help minimise problems. As soon as pests and diseases become apparent they should be treated. If insect infestations are caught early enough they can be easily removed by hand and crushed, or drowned or disposed in some other way. Diseased leaves or stems can be simply removed and then burnt. You must be careful, however, and wash your hands after handling diseased material—fungal spores can be inadvertently spread to other plants.

Natural predators should be encouraged in your garden, particularly birds. Parasitic bacteria that attack only moths and caterpillars can be purchased as a spray known as Dipel. Parasitic spider mites that attack and control red spider can also be purchased from a number of companies.

If problems are too large to cope with by hand then you may have to use a 'safe' spray; chemical sprays should be particularly avoided on culinary and medicinal herbs. Many commercial sprays are based on naturally occurring plant products such as garlic, pyrethrum, eucalyptus oil, etc. Other safe sprays include products based on liquid soaps, such as Clensel, or on mineral oils such as white oil.

Sodium bicarbonate, a common cooking ingredient, has been found to protect beans, cucumbers and muskmelons from fungi. It may be worth trying on herbs which suffer from fungal attack. A spray of one part well-rotted compost to six parts water that is allowed to stand for a week and then filtered has worked well against blights, anthracnose and some mildews in West German university trials.

## Hydroponic herbs

Hydroponics is the technique of growing plants without soil. The roots grow either in air, directly in water, or in a sterile solid material. Nutrients are periodically added to the roots as a solution.

If this sounds too complicated for you, it really isn't. Herbs have been grown successfully in hydroponics both by home gardeners and commercial growers, and a lot of fun can be had doing so.

Perhaps the greatest advantage of hydroponics is that it saves the back-breaking work of gardening in the ground. Weeds are eliminated, digging is avoided, pests and diseases are reduced and if you want, the beds can be set at waist height so you don't even have to bend over.

## Getting Started

One of the easiest ways to get started is with gravel culture:

1. Fill a container (e.g. a large tub or pot) with coarse washed gravel or sand.
2. Remove the herbs from their pots and wash all the soil from the roots under a running tap.
3. Plant the herbs into the gravel or sand, being careful to avoid damaging the roots.
4. Mix up a hydroponic nutrient solution. (This can be obtained from any hydroponic supplier—see under Hydroponics in the yellow pages of your phone book.) Alternatively make your own solution: mix 5 parts gypsum and 1 part epsom salts added to 6 parts of powdered soluble plant food such as Thrive, Aquasol or Phostrogen. Water the gravel until it is thoroughly wet and excess water is draining through the bottom of the container.
5. Water the herbs with the nutrient solution whenever the soil is dry.

There is a wide range of hydroponic systems on the market, some even do the watering and feeding automatically. All that is left for you to do is watch your herbs grow!

Suitable herbs to grow in hydroponics:

| Basil | Thyme | Oregano |
| Chervil | Mint | Chives |
| Parsley | Marjoram | Watercress |
| Sage | | |

For more information on hydroponics read *Commercial Hydroponics* by John Mason, published by Kangaroo Press, available from John Mason, 264 Swansea Rd, Lilydale, Victoria, Australia, 3140.

# 2 Landscaping with Herbs

Herbs can be used in many different ways in the garden. A separate 'herb garden' is of course something special and is potentially a stunning feature. However, herbs don't have to be segregated from the rest of your plants. Most herbs are very hardy and adaptable plants which will grow happily in containers or garden beds throughout the rest of the garden.

There are herbs to suit every garden situation. They can be grown in full sun or shade, in wet or dry soil, and include trees, shrubs, climbers and ground covers. You can find a herb for every situation if you look hard enough.

## Using Herbs With Other Plants

If you plan to intersperse herbs throughout the garden, choose your plants carefully to avoid herbs which might 'take over'. All too often, what started as a very desirable plant ends up becoming a weed. There are two ways this problem can develop:

1. Suckering herbs like mint and sorrel simply take root and send up shoots over an ever-increasing area. Suckering herbs can either be grown in containers or confined to part of a garden bed by building an underground barrier around the plant roots. To create an underground barrier, cut the bottom out of a 30–50 cm tall plastic tub or rubbish bin, dig a hole 30–50 cm deep and sit the container in the hole with the top projecting about 1 cm above the soil surface. The centre is then filled in with the previously dug soil and the herb is planted in the centre. You will still need to keep a close eye on the herb, but it will be much easier to confine.

Invasive weeds can also be kept apart by the following methods:

### a) Segmented beds
Divide a bed into sections by making below-ground walls to stop roots spreading from one area to the next. This can be achieved using timber sleepers, bricks, concrete edging and plastic strips (there is a variety of commercial plastic edgings available).

Another popular method is to bury short, large diameter ceramic or concrete pipes in the ground so that the top of the pipe projects just above soil level. Vigorous herbs can also be confined to pocket plantings in rockeries with deep barriers of rock or concrete extending into the soil on all sides of the herb.

### b) Raised beds
A series of beds is created above the soil level by building walls and filling in with soil. Herbs of similar vigour are planted in each bed.

Common invasive suckering herbs are jasmine, honeysuckle, hot mint, common mint, eau de cologne mint, pennyroyal and scented geraniums.

2. Herbs like evening primrose and lemon balm drop large quantities of seed which, under the right con-

19

**Step 1**

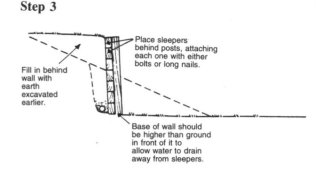

original soil level

remove soil from here

place soil here

**Step 2**

The sleeper post should lean slightly backwards towards the high side of the embankment.

Lay an agricultural drainage pipe behind the wall to take water away. Cover with loose stones.

Set sleeper posts in concrete foundations (at least 1/5 of the length of the sleeper should be set in concrete).

**Step 3**

Place sleepers behind posts, attaching each one with either bolts or long nails.

Fill in behind wall with earth excavated earlier.

Base of wall should be higher than ground in front of it to allow water to drain away from sleepers.

ditions, sprout wherever they drop. The only way to prevent this problem is to either cut the flowers off before the seeds form or simply avoid planting this type of invasive herb.

A large range of herbs are non-invasive and fit in well with most common garden shrubs. You will have few problems integrating lavender, southern-wood, wormwood, thyme, lemon verbena, rose and rosemary in your garden.

# Planning Your Herb Garden

There are four stages to planning a herb garden:

1. Decide what you want

Why do you want herbs in your garden? Decide what herbs you want to grow and how much space you will devote to herbs.

Are you going to plant all of your herbs together, or will you scatter them throughout the garden? Decide which parts of your property best suit which herbs. Most herbs like a well-drained soil and full or filtered sunlight, although some herbs will grow in wet areas (e.g. mints). Dry areas may need to be mulched or irrigated.

2. Survey the site and draw a base plan

You will need a base plan of your garden area to draw on. Often a builder's plan can be traced over or enlarged using a photocopier. The plan should be drawn to scale and show buildings, fences, existing walls, paths, underground pipes, etc. If you can't obtain an old plan, you will need to measure the site and draw your own base plan. A good scale to work on is 1:100 (i.e. this means that for every 100 cm or 1 m in 'real life', you should draw 1 cm on your plan).

3. Draw in the main features

Make a couple of copies of your base plan which show the site as it now exists, including all of the permanent features such as the house, carport, garden shed and water tanks (if you have them). Now let your imagination go and draw in the major features of your new design (i.e. paths, garden beds, walls, paving, fences, water, lawn, etc.). Try placing them in a few different ways. Don't worry about the details at this stage; just look at the broad picture.

Take a few days to consider your drawings before settling on a final layout, then draw in these main features on your plan.

4. Draw in the plants

Use a pencil to fill in the detail showing what plants

Designing a Herb Garden

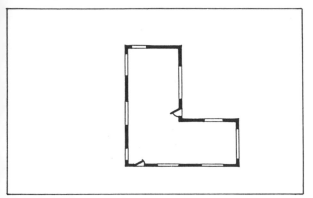

1. Draw the property as it now exists.

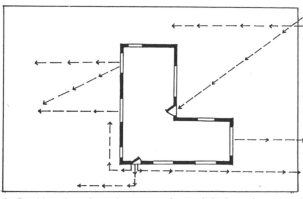

2. Consider where the main access points and the best views are. These can be developed as pathways and focal points.

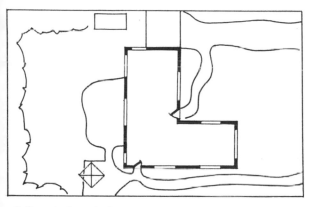

3. Draw in the main features.

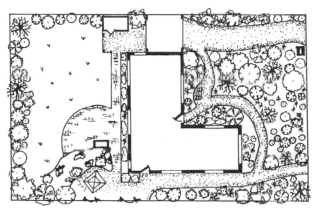

4. Fill in the final details.

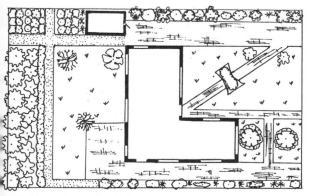

5. Alternative garden designs.

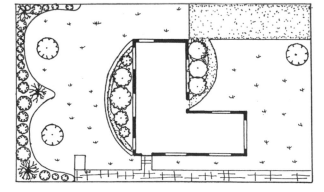

should go where. Again, take a few days to consider your design. Talk to your partner or a friend about the pros and cons of your selection and arrangement of plants. Adjust your design a few times until you are satisfied.

Remember to allow for the future growth of the plants. You will eventually lose some of your plants through overcrowding if the plants are grown too close together or vigorous plants are placed too close to weaker-growing plants.

# Planting Design

When you choose your plants you need to take many things into consideration. Consider the following points:

• Position each plant where it will grow well. Soil, light and other conditions should be appropriate for the plant's needs.
• Grow enough of each plant to meet your needs (culinary, craft, medicinal, cosmetic, etc).
• Grow plants together which are good companions (i.e. which have a beneficial effect on each other—see chapter 3).
• Group plants together which have a similar vigour. Vigorous plants can smother weaker-growing neighbours.
• Avoid growing too many plants which flower in the same season.
• Avoid growing too many deciduous or seasonal perennials which will leave bare patches in the garden during winter.
• Try to achieve contrast in foliage colour and texture. (Don't put two plants with a similar appearance side by side.)
• Remember tall-growing plants will eventually create shade for plants growing near them.
• Ensure plants which you will harvest frequently are accessible—you don't want to damage other herbs as you try to get through to the one you want. Stepping stones conveniently placed in the garden bed can be a useful way of overcoming this problem.
• Place fragrant plants near pathways or patios. They will release their perfume as people brush past them.

# How many herbs should I grow?

Herbs can become either a small or large part of a home garden, depending on two things:

1. The requirements of the household for herbs to use in cooking, crafts, medicines, etc.
2. The preference which the home owner has for herbs above other plants.

It is not much use growing large quantities of just one or two herbs. You will probably soon get tired of those particular herbs and, unless you are giving away lots to your friends and neighbours or selling your excess produce, you are wasting valuable garden space. Try growing smaller amounts of a wide variety of herbs. Of course a little extra space can be used for growing your 'favourites'.

If only a few different types of herbs are required for cooking—perhaps parsley, mint, chives and garlic—they can be grown in a corner of the garden, in part of the vegetable garden, or perhaps in containers. More serious herb gardeners though will want to devote special areas of the garden for growing herbs, perhaps by creating a series of herb beds with paths between them.

# Some types of herb gardens

## Formal herb gardens

Almost any geometric form can be used to create a formal herb garden, although the bed should be symmetrically arranged on two sides of a central line or axis. The central line normally extends from a doorway, gate or other point of entry into the herb garden.

The central axis forms a line along which the eye is drawn, and as such, an interesting feature is usually located at the end and/or in the centre of the axis. Popular features are fountains, sundials, arbours, topiary and statues.

Formal herb gardens should consist of well-defined lines. Low walls, finely-cut edges and hedges are ideal for edging beds in a formal garden.

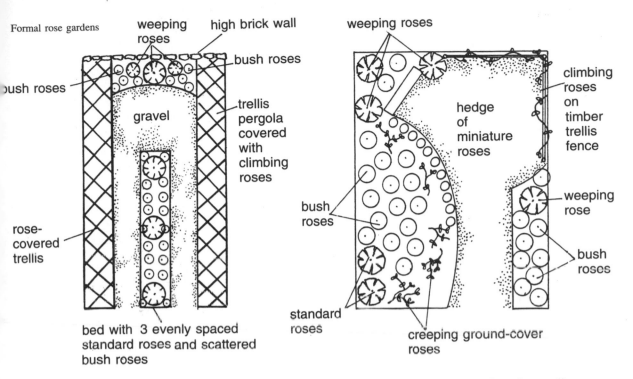

Formal rose gardens

weeping roses

high brick wall

bush roses

bush roses

gravel

trellis pergola covered with climbing roses

weeping roses

hedge of miniature roses

climbing roses on timber trellis fence

bush roses

rose-covered trellis

weeping rose

bush roses

standard roses

bed with 3 evenly spaced standard roses and scattered bush roses

creeping ground-cover roses

## The perennial border

Many herbs are perennial plants which grow strongly throughout the warmer months and die back to their root systems in winter.

A garden bed made up of evergreen trees and shrubs is often planted with a strip of seasonal perennial plants edging the lawn or path. These plants grow strongly during spring and summer and fill the garden bed in the warmer months. When the plants die back in winter they leave a bare strip, creating a more spacious appearance in the garden.

Ideal herbs for a perennial border include apple mint, lemon balm, bergamot, fennel, angelica, sage, tansy, yarrow, chives, Russian garlic and hyssop.

## Rock gardens

Many herbs suit rock gardens because they grow well in confined spaces and can tolerate fluctuating water levels in the soil. You need to be aware of the vigour of different types of herbs though. The danger in a rock garden is that one type of herb might take over and compete to the detriment of other plants in the bed. The following herbs are particularly suited to grow in a rockery:

| Plant | Colour | Height | Comments |
|---|---|---|---|
| Betony | Purple spring flowers | 60 cm | Rich moist soil, sun to semi-shade |
| Bugle | Bronze leaves, spring flowers | 2 cm | Very hardy, can be invasive |
| Chives | Pink flowers in spring | 15 cm | Clump-forming; needs moist but well-drained soil |
| Columbine | Yellow flowers in spring | 70 cm | Fern-like foliage |
| Curry plant | Yellow flowers in summer, grey foliage | 60 cm | Dwarf form also available |

| Plant | Colour | Height | Comments |
|---|---|---|---|
| Dianthus | Spring flowers, grey foliage | 2-5 cm | Forms compact mats, not very invasive |
| Golden lemon thyme | Yellow foliage | to 10 cm | Spreading, not invasive |
| Italian lavender | Rich purple flowers, blue-grey foliage | 30 cm | Compact shrub with narrow leaves |
| Lamb's ears | Woolly grey foliage | 4–6 cm | Can be mildly invasive |
| Lavender cotton | Grey foliage, yellow flowers | 20 cm | Dense, rounded shrub, prune annually to maintain vigour |
| Lemon geranium | Small variegated leaves | 60 cm | One of the smaller scented geraniums; can be pruned to keep even smaller. |
| Creeping rosemary | Blue flowers, dark foliage | 10 cm | Spreading but not invasive |
| Winter savory | Pink, lilac to white flowers | 30 cm | Leaves used commercially to flavour salami |
| Yarrow | Attractive white, pink or red flowers | 20 cm | Fine fern-like foliage; can be invasive |

## How to Build a Rockery

A rockery only looks good if the rocks and plants look as though they naturally belong there. Before building a rockery, take a drive or a walk and look at the way rocks occur in the bush. Note how plants grow amongst rocks alongside creeks and rivers and in crevices on mountains and hillsides.

When you build a rockery, remember the following points:
• Always bury at least 50% of the rock.
• Place the rocks so that they touch each other.
• Expose the most weathered surface and bury any surfaces which have been marked by machinery or cracked by blasting.
• Build the rockery on sloping ground. If you don't have a slope, build a slight mound.
• Use larger rocks at the bottom of the mound and smaller rocks higher up.
• Allow plants to partially spread over the rocks. Occasional pruning may be needed to keep some of the rocks visible.
• Ensure there is good drainage under the rockery. In heavy soils you may need to install agricultural drainage pipes before placing the rocks.

## The Cottage Garden

The cottage garden concept involves planting perennials and herbs together, perhaps along with fruit trees and maybe some old world shrubs to create a potpourri effect. This may sound like a mess, but in reality is well thought out to achieve a blend of textures and colours which will be attractive at all times of the year. Mixing plants in this way also creates symbiotic relationships between adjacent plants (i.e. they complement the health of each other rather than competing or damaging each other).

## Xeriscape gardens

A xeriscape is a garden which is specifically designed to contain plants with similar water requirements. For example, a typical xeriscape would be a herb garden which uses ten different herbs which are all drought-resistant and, under normal conditions, only like to be watered sparsely.

Many herbs are excellent candidates for xeriscape gardens. Most culinary herbs can be grown in areas that receive only 5 cm of water per month.

Good indicators of herbs suited to xeriscapes are leaf colour and place of origin. Herbs with small silver-coloured leaves and herbs which originate from the Mediterranean region are likely to tolerate hot dry conditions, e.g. rosemary, thyme, santolina and sage.

Another indication of drought tolerance is the presence of a long tap root, e.g. comfrey, fennel and parsley. The bulbous herbs like chives, garlic and saffron crocus have built-in water storage. Aloe has succulent leaves for this same purpose. Other drought-tolerant herbs are catnip, lavender, pennyroyal, rue, yarrow and bay laurel.

By growing plants together which have similar requirements for water, your task of looking after them is made much easier. Plants that require water during extreme heat can be mulched and grouped together closer to the house or water supply, while plants which can survive on natural rainfall can be placed in areas of extreme exposure such as a west or south-facing bank.

Annual herbs should be frequently watered when first planted; watering should then be tapered off to encourage the plants to develop strong, deep root systems. Water deeply and infrequently rather than in short bursts. This helps avoid encouraging the root system to develop in the top soil.

If herbs look strong and vigorous, do not water. Brown leaf tips are not serious, nor is slight drooping during hot parts of the day. If herbs have not recovered at dusk, then you should water them. Herbs grown in drier conditions are less attractive to insects and have a stronger concentration of aromatic oils.

*Herbs to use in xeriscapes*

| | | |
|---|---|---|
| Artemisia | Jerusalem | Tansy |
| Betony | sage | Teasel |
| Catnip | Lavender | Thyme |
| Chamomile | Marjoram | Vervain |
| Coreopsis | Musk mallow | Winter savory |
| Evening | Rosemary | Yarrow |
| primrose | Rue | |
| Fennel | St. John's | |
| Horehound | wort | |
| Hyssop | Salad burnet | |

## Topiary

Topiary involves pruning plants into shapes such as balls, pillars, pyramids, arches, or even animals and buildings.

There are two different ways to create a topiary:

1. Make a framework out of metal or wire and grow the plant over the frame, pruning it to the shape of the frame.

You can create simple wire frames by bending thick wire with the aid of pliers. To create circular shapes, bend wire around a large tub or barrel.

One of the simplest forms is a wire circle on top of a straight pole: use a wooden stake for the pole and tie the wire circle to the top. More complex shapes such as animals can be bought pre-made from some of the 'boutique style' garden shops in larger cities.

Climbing or creeping herbs are the best plants to train on wire frames. Hollow wire mesh frames are sometimes filled with moss which is kept moist to support the growth of creeping plants such as Corsican mint or pennyroyal.

Plants suited to topiary on wire frames include ivy, honeysuckle, mints, pennyroyal, prostrate rosemary, thyme, curry plant and lavender cotton.

2. Train a plant from an early stage by pruning (and staking, if support is needed). Generally, woody herbs are preferred for this method of training.

Plants suited to topiary without a frame include bay laurel, cypress, *Buxus* (English box), lavender, scented geraniums, rosemary, rose, *Myrtus*, *Salvia officinalis*, pineapple sage and lemon verbena.

Whatever method you use, frequent pruning is the key to achieving a good topiary. Once a topiary gets too far out of shape, it can be almost impossible to return to the original form.

## Hedges

Hedges are commonly used to border herb gardens. Plant hedging plants at a distance apart which is half or less of the intended height of the hedge.

Hedges should always have a slight taper from the top to the bottom (i.e. the bottom of the hedge should be wider than the top to allow the bottom to receive ample light).

As with plants grown in topiary, hedges must be pruned regularly. With many types of plants (conifers in particular), pruning too heavily into old wood can cause die-back, leaving a permanent dead patch in the hedge.

When buying plants for a hedge, always get a few

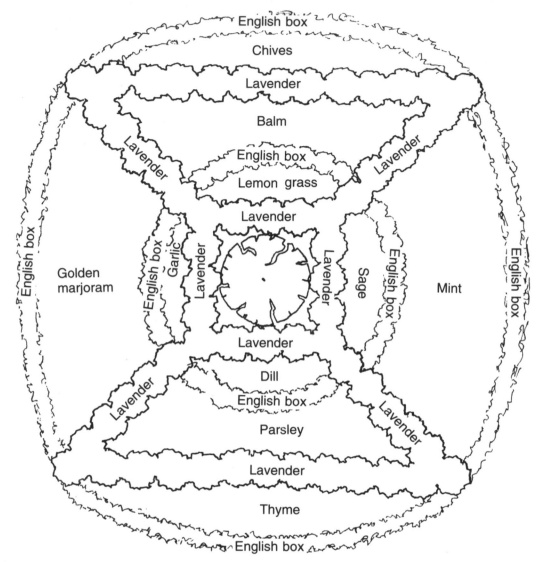

English box
Chives
Lavender
Balm
English box
Lemon grass
Lavender
Lavender
Lavender
Dill
English box
Parsley
Lavender
Thyme
English box

Lavender
Lavender

English box
English box
Golden marjoram
English box
Garlic
Lavender
Sage
English box
Mint
English box

Lavender
Lavender

Simple herb knot garden using hedges to divide sections of
different herbs

extras in case the odd plant dies. Pot up the extras
and keep them healthy and in reserve.

Plants suited to tall hedges include bay laurel,
lavender, *Lonicera nitida*, rosemary, lavender cotton,
sage, scented geranium, southernwood and
wormwood.

Plants suited to low hedges include *Artemisia*
(dwarf types), currant, lavender (dwarf types), curry
plant, catnip, ivy, germander, hyssop, lavender
cotton, common thyme and winter savory.

## Variations

Stilt hedge: the stem of each hedge plant is pruned
bare (like a standard rose) up to a certain height, then
a solid hedge of vegetation is trained on top. The
finished result is a hedge which appears to be sitting
up in the air on top of evenly spaced posts.

Hedge embellishments: a topiary is developed on top
of the hedge. Simple embellishments are raised balls
or domes on top of the hedge at evenly spaced intervals. More complex embellishments can be created in
shapes such as animals or anything you desire.

# Ideas of how to plant your herbs

## Spiral

After cultivating the soil, dig a spiral-shaped furrow. Plant seeds of one type of herb in the furrow to create a spiralling 'hedge' of plants. Other herbs can then be planted in the spaces between the furrow.

## Maze

A maze doesn't have to cover a large area, nor does the hedge barrier have to be tall. Interesting hedges can be as low-growing as 0.3–1 m. Try designing a small maze using one or more different herbs as a low hedge. Suitable hedge plants include lavender cotton, lavender, wormwood, southernwood, rosemary and juniper.

## Tyre garden

Place disused car tyres on the ground and fill them and the gaps between them with soil or compost. Plant a different herb in each tyre. The rubber walls between each herb will help prevent competition between different types of herbs. The tyre beds also provide improved drainage, and the tyre rubber makes a nice soft, safe material that minimises the risk of children hurting themselves or of machines such as mowers being damaged.

## Raised beds

Build a rock or wooden sleeper wall around a garden bed and fill the centre with soil or compost. Even if the bed is only 10 cm above the normal soil level, drainage will be improved enough to grow a wide range of herbs which prefer drier soils (e.g. the Mediterranean herbs).

## Herb pots

Herb pots are usually made from terracotta and have planting holes in the sides as well as in the top. These allow several different herbs to be planted in the one pot while keeping the foliage of each plant separated.

## Hanging baskets

Many herbs can be successfully grown in hanging baskets although the soil will dry out quickly, so either be prepared to do lots of watering or use drought-tolerant herbs.

## Features and focal points

The eye is always drawn to something different. Try putting an interesting feature in the centre or at the end of a garden. An urn, sundial, fountain, seat, gazebo or even a different coloured tree or large shrub can be used in this way.

Consider the lines along which the feature will be viewed. If a feature is at the end of a long path, keep the view clear—don't plant overhanging trees or shrubs. You could install a garden arch, build a garden wall, or plant a hedge to frame the feature. The feature can still be seen through the opening, but the surroundings are blocked so they don't detract from the feature.

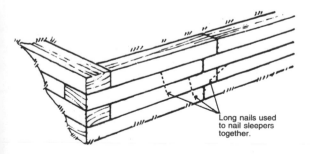

Long nails used to nail sleepers together.

Sleeper wall constructed with sleepers laid on side

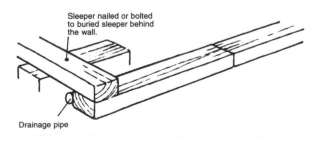

Sleeper nailed or bolted to buried sleeper behind the wall.

Drainage pipe

Method of fixing wall into mound behind

# Colourful and Fragrant Herb Gardens

Gardens are a delight at any time, but never more so than when in full bloom and enriched by fragrances. All too often these are temporary highlights rather than permanent characteristics of a garden. By carefully selecting herbs, however, you can have a continuously changing array of colours and fragrances to delight your senses.

We usually think of colour and scent coming from the flowers, but that isn't always the case. Foliage, bark and fruits can also be colourful or scented. Consider, for example, conifers or gum trees which have their own characteristic aromas, irrespective of the time of year; the colourful berries on a cotoneaster; the fruit on an apple tree; and the rich autumn foliage of deciduous trees.

Flowers normally release their perfume without being touched, but leaves and other plant parts often need to be brushed or bruised to release their scented oils. The scent from many fragrant flowers is strongest in the early evening, particularly on hot days when the sun's warmth will strengthen the perfumes. Consider where you are likely to be sitting in the early evening, on warm nights. A summer patio, for instance, may be an appropriate place to plant evening-scented plants.

Scents may also not always be fragrant. Some scents are very pungent or offensive and certain scents may create allergy problems.

## Guidelines for Planning a Fragrant Garden

• Don't grow too many varieties of strongly-scented plants close together. The fragrance can become overpowering and the different scents might not blend together well.
• Don't grow strongly-scented plants close to those with subtle scents. A subtle fragrance can be totally overwhelmed by a stronger scent.
• Avoid planting strongly-scented plants in enclosed, poorly ventilated areas. Strong scents need to be moved by the wind. If confined, they can become overpowering.
• Consider the prevailing winds and remember that the scent will move in the direction of the wind.
• Grow plants with scented foliage near living areas such as patios and verandahs, or near pathways and drives where overhanging branches can be brushed as people or vehicles pass by.
• Fragrant lawn species will also release scents when walked upon or mown. For wet lawns, try pennyroyal and peppermint; for drier lawns, try chamomile.
• Scented plants can often be grown in pots and other containers. These can be moved into different positions as desired, for example, you can move a plant close to a living area when it is strongly in scent and move it away at other times.

Annuals and perennials with fragrant flowers include *Asperula odorata*, *Centaurea moschata*, *Cheiranthus cheirei* (wallflower), carnation, chrysanthemum, *Corydalis lutea*, *Dianthus* (pinks), *Heliotropium* (heliotrope), *Lathyrus* (sweet pea), *Lupinus* (lupin), *Matthiola* (stock), *Monarda didyma* (bergamot), *Myosotis sylvatica* (forget-me-not), primroses, pansies and violas.

Annual and perennial herbs can be planted in any of the following arrangements:

1. In a series of tiers
A row of low-growing herbs to 10 or 15 cm tall is used as a border. Behind this is grown a row of taller plants and behind that another row of even taller plants.
2. Rows with dot plants
Tall plants are scattered at random rising above a carpet of lower-growing plants.
3. Clumping
Herbs are grown in clumps amongst other clumps of perennials or annuals; as 'fillers' between woody shrubs in a permanent garden bed; or in pockets in a rockery.
4. Single variety scheme
The bed is planted with colourful herbs of the same variety, e.g. blue-flowering violets.

## Lemon-scented Herbs

The wonderfully refreshing scent of lemon is a welcome addition to any garden. This scent can be readily supplied by a surprising number of herbs.

**Lemon-scented Herbs At a Glance**

| Herb | Plant Type | Size | Uses | | | Propagation |
| --- | --- | --- | --- | --- | --- | --- |
| | | | Culinary | Tea | Ornamental | |
| Lemon verbena | Medium shrub | 3 m | x | x | x | Cuttings |
| Lemon balm | Small perennial | 60 cm | x | x | | Seed, cuttings |
| Lemon thyme | Small perennial | 25–30 cm | x | x | x | Cuttings, division |
| Lemon-scented darwinia | Small shrub | 60 cm | | | x | Cuttings |
| Scented geraniums | Small shrub | 1 m | x | x | x | Cuttings, seed |
| Lemon-scented tea tree | Med. shrub | 4 m | | x | x | Cuttings, seed |
| Lemon grass | Perennial grass | 2 m | x | x | x | Division |
| Lemon basil | Annual | 60 cm | x | | x | Seed, cuttings |
| Lemon mint | Annual | 60 cm | x | x | x | Cuttings, division |
| Lemon catnip | Small perennial | 1 m | | x | x | Seed, cuttings |
| Lemon-scented gum | Large tree | 30 m+ | | | x | Seed |
| *Backhousia citriodora* | Med. tree | 15 m | | | x | Cuttings |

# Choosing Herbs for Special Effects and Situations

## Blue/Grey foliage

Agrimony
Apple mint
Artichoke (globe)
Blue gum
Catmint
Catnip
Clary sage
*Coleus caninus*
Costmary
Curry plant
Dianthus
Five-seasons herb
Germander
Horehound
Lamb's ears
Lavender
Marshmallow
Mugwort
Peppermint-scented geranium
Rue
Sage
Santolina
Southernwood
Woolly thyme
Wormwood
Yarrow

## Gold/Variegated foliage forms

Apple mint
Comfrey
Five-seasons herb
Golden marjoram
Honeywort
Hot mint
*Juniperus communis* (gold forms)
Lemon balm
Lemon-scented pelargonium
Nasturtium (some varieties)
Sage
Silver thyme
Variegated lemon thyme

## Purple foliage

Basil (purple and red form)
Bronze fennel
Bugle
Castor oil plant
Herb robert
Hot mint
Fennel (bronze type)
Sage (purple form)

## White flowers

Anise
Apple mint
Basil (sweet)
Caraway
Chamomile
Chervil
Feverfew
Garlic
Garlic chives
Hyssop
Lily-of-the-valley
Nutmeg geranium
Peppermint-scented geranium
Valerian (common)
White lavender
Winter savory
Yarrow

## Yellow or cream flowers

Anise
Angelica
Agrimony
Arnica
Broom
Coltsfoot
Cowslip
Dandelion
Dill
Elecampane
Evening primrose
Fennel
Honeysuckle
Lovage
Mullein
Mustard
Pot marigold
Pregnant onion
Santolina
Sunflower
Tansy
Yarrow
Yellow flag iris

## Purple foliage

| | | |
|---|---|---|
| Bergamot (wild) | Dyer's chamomile | Sage |
| Betony | Hyssop | Scullcap |
| Chives | Lavender | Vervain |
| Clary sage | Lobelia | Violet |
| Comfrey | Mint | |

## Pink flowers

| | | |
|---|---|---|
| Centaury | Hollyhock | Red valerian |
| Coriander | Marshmallow | Rose |
| Cumin | Motherwort | Soapwort |
| Cinnamon geranium | Oregano | Thyme |
| | Pink hyssop | Yarrow |
| Coconut geranium | Pink lavender | |
| | Pot marjoram | |
| Foxglove | Red clover | |

## Blue flowers

| | | |
|---|---|---|
| Borage | Hyssop | Rosemary |
| Chicory | Larkspur | Sea holly |
| Columbine | *Lavandula lanata* | |
| Gentian (blue) | | |
| Germander | | |

## Red flowers

| | | |
|---|---|---|
| Bergamot | Poppy | Salad burnet |
| Crimson clover | Red valerian | |

## Drought-resistant herbs

| | | |
|---|---|---|
| Bee balm | Feverfew | Rue |
| Betony | Dyer's broom | Rose |
| Broom | Evening primrose | Salad burnet |
| Calamint | | Statice |
| Catnip | Fennel | Sweet woodruff |
| Costmary | Hyssop | |
| Creeping thyme | Jerusalem sage | Vervain |
| | Lavender | Winter savory |
| Curry plant | Marjoram | Woad |
| Dianthus | Rosemary | |

| | | | |
|---|---|---|---|
| 1 Citrus | 4 Rosemary | 8 Lemon Verbena | 11 Chives |
| 2 Scented geranium | 5 Wormwood | | 12 Thyme |
| | 6 Comfrey | 9 Rose bush | 13 Bergamot |
| 3 French lavender | 7 Sage | 10 Golden Marjoram | |

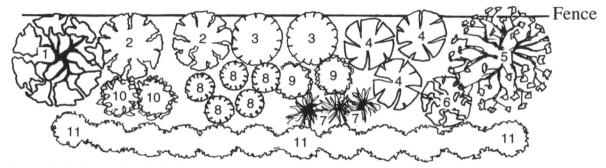

Herb border for well-drained but moist soil.

| | |
|---|---|
| 1 Lemon tree | 7 Yarrow |
| 2 Wormwood | 8 Lemon balm |
| 3 Rosemary | 9 Pineapple sage |
| 4 Scented geranium | 10 Tansy |
| 5 Bay laurel | 11 Lavender hedge |
| 6 Mullein | |

Herb border for dry or well-drained soil.

## Very drought-resistant herbs

| | | |
|---|---|---|
| Mullein | Sumac (*Rhus* | Wormwood |
| Mugwort | spp.) | Yarrow |
| Santolina | Southernwood | |
| Russian sage | Tansy | |
| (*Perovskia* | Woolly thyme | |
| *atriplicifolia*) | | |

## Herbs which grow in wet soils

| | | |
|---|---|---|
| Angelica | Mints (all | Pennyroyal |
| Bergamot | except | Sweet flag |
| Comfrey | catnip) | Valerian |
| Lady's mantle | Parsley | Violet |
| Lovage | | |

## Ground-covering herbs

| | | |
|---|---|---|
| Bugle | Lady's | Savory (some |
| Chamomile | bedstraw | types) |
| (Roman) | Lamb's ears | Sorrel |
| Clover | Nasturtium | Sweet |
| Corsican mint | Pennyroyal | woodruff |
| Germander | Peppermint- | Thyme (several |
| (creeping | scented | types) |
| form) | geranium | Violet |
| Golden | Rosemary | Yarrow |
| marjoram | (prostrate | |
| Ground ivy | type) | |
| *Juniperus com-* | | |
| *munis* (pros- | | |
| trate types) | | |

## Climbers

| | | |
|---|---|---|
| Honeysuckle | Jasmine | Rose (climbing |
| Hop | Passion flower | types) |

## Narrow-leaved herbs

| | | |
|---|---|---|
| Chives | Lemon grass | Shallots |
| Garlic | Onion | |

## Trees

| | | |
|---|---|---|
| Bay laurel | Hawthorn | Tea tree |
| Citrus | *Juniperus com-* | Witch hazel |
| Cinnamon | *munis* (tree | |
| Eucalypts | forms) | |
| Ginkgo | | |

## Herbs which grow in tropical conditions

| | | |
|---|---|---|
| Aloe | Comfrey | Oregano |
| Angelica | Coriander | Parsley |
| Anise | Fennel | Pennyroyal |
| Basil | Five-seasons | Potentilla |
| Bee balm | herb | Rosemary |
| Burdock | Foxglove | Rue |
| Calendula | Garlic | Salad burnet |
| Cardamom | Ginger | Scented |
| Castor oil plant | Germander | geranium |
| Capsicum | Lavender | Soapwort |
| Citrus | (some types) | Southernwood |
| Chamomile | Lemon scented | Sunflower |
| (both Roman | gum | Sweet flag |
| and German) | Lobelia | Thyme |
| Cinnamon | Marjoram | Wormwood |
| Cloves (*Syzy-* | Mint (most | |
| *gium* | types) | |
| *aromaticum*) | Myrtle | |
| Coffee | Nasturtium | |

## Spicy-scented herbs

| | | |
|---|---|---|
| Anise | Cardamom | Pennyroyal |
| Basil | Coriander | Spice-scented |
| Caraway | Mint | geranium |

## Earthy-scented herbs

| | | |
|---|---|---|
| Chamomile | Marjoram | Southernwood |
| Clary sage | Pine | Thyme |
| Eucalyptus | Rosemary | Wormwood |
| Lady's | Savory | |
| bedstraw | | |

## Herbs for shaded places

| | | |
|---|---|---|
| Alpine | Germander | Orris |
|   strawberry | Golden | Parsley |
| Angelica |   marjoram | Primula |
| Balm of Gilead | Good King | Rosemary |
| Betony |   Henry | Sorrel |
| Bugle | Lily-of-the- | Sweet |
| Capsicum |   valley |   woodruff |
| Catmint | Lady's mantle | Wormwood |
| Chives | Lovage | Violet |
| Chervil | Mint | |
| Comfrey | Nasturtium | |

## Herbs to grow in shade in tropical areas

| | | |
|---|---|---|
| Bee balm | Germander | Rosemary |
| Cardamom | Ginger | Salad burnet |
| Castor oil plant | Lobelia | Soapwort |
| Capsicum | Mint | Thyme |
| Comfrey | Parsley | Vietnamese |
| Foxglove | Pennyroyal |   mint |
| Garlic | Periwinkle | Wormwood |

## Floral-scented herbs

| | | |
|---|---|---|
| Gardenia | Lavender | Rose |
| Honeysuckle | Lilac | Scented |
| Hyacinth | Lily-of-the- |   geranium |
| Jasmine |   valley | Violet |

## Herbs for hedges

| | | |
|---|---|---|
| Curry plant | Lavender | Sage |
| English box |   cotton |   (common) |
| Germander | Lavender | Southernwood |
|   (tall | *Lonicera nitida* | Wormwood |
| varieties) | Marjoram | |
| Hyssop | Rosemary | |
| Jerusalem sage | | |

Raised beds in the herb garden in Melbourne Botanic Gardens look good and provide plants with excellent drainage.

A herb garden built around garden steps on a slope at Montville in Queensland.

Yellow-flowering rue dominates the herb garden at Churchill Island, Victoria. An informal and relatively inexpensive herb garden, with gravel paths and plants scattered irregularly throughout garden beds.

The cottage and herb garden at Ashcombe Maze on the Mornington Peninsula near Melbourne. With herbs and perennial plants a garden like this can be established in as little as 12 months.

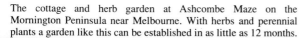

*Aloe vera*

Basil (*Ocimum basilicum*)
Bergamot (*Monarda didyma*)

Angelica (*Angelica archangelica*)
Bay tree (*Laurus nobilis*)

# 3  Companion Planting

Companion planting is a natural progression for anyone interested in growing herbs. Most herb gardeners prefer using chemical-free methods to control pests and diseases—companion plants can be an effective and natural way of combatting these problems.

In companion planting plants are grown together to provide certain benefits to each other. The benefits these plant associations offer include the attraction of beneficial insects to the garden, which may act as predators to harmful pests, or pollinators to surrounding flowers; the repelling of harmful insects and diseases through the secretions of aromatic oils; and an improvement in soil fertility and structure.

Marigolds are grown as companion plants to deter nematodes.

## Companion Planting Table

| Plant | Companion | Comments |
| --- | --- | --- |
| Apple | Chives | Less chance of apple scab disease |
| Apple | Wormwood, garlic | Protects apple from codling moth |
| Apple | Tobacco | Deters aphis and thrips on apple |
| Asparagus | Parsley | Asparagus becomes more vigorous |
| Bean | Marigold, petunia | Beetles are repelled from beans |
| Bean | Summer savory | Beans grow more strongly |
| Beetroot | Onion | Beetroot grows better |
| Black currants | Wormwood | Prevents rust disease on currants |
| Broccoli | Dill, mint | Broccoli grows better |
| Cabbage | Rosemary, sage | Repels cabbage butterfly |

| Plant | Companion | Comments | Plant | Companion | Comments |
|-------|-----------|----------|-------|-----------|----------|
| Cabbage | Celeriac, celery | Helps control grubs on cabbage | Lettuce | Chervil | Deters aphis, snails and mildew |
| Caraway | Pea, bean, lettuce, onion, carrot | Sown together, caraway seed germination is improved | Onion | Chamomile | Improves flavour of onions |
| Carrot | Sage, onion | Carrot fly is repelled | Peach | Garlic | Reduces chance of peach leaf curl disease |
| Carrot | Dill | Chemicals secreted by dill improve health of carrots | Potato | Horseradish | Increases disease resistance in potatoes |
| Celery | Bush bean | Help each other grow better | Potato | Beans | Potatoes less likely to suffer beetle damage |
| Coriander | Anise, radish, spinach | Coriander germinates and develops faster | Potato | French lavender | Controls nematodes |
| Corn | Bean, pea | Provide increased nitrogen supply to corn (plant the peas or beans in alternate rows) | Pumpkin | Datura | Pumpkin vigour and health is increased |
|  |  |  | Radish | Lettuce | In summer radishes are more succulent |
|  |  |  | Raspberries | Rue | Controls Japanese beetle |
| Corn | Sunflower | Incidence of armyworm decreases | Rose | Chives, garlic | Protects from black spot and some pests including aphids |
| Eggplant | Amaranthus | Less likelihood of insects on eggplant | Rose | Parsley | Protects rose from leaf-eating beetles |
| Eggplant | Beans | Beetles repelled from eggplant | Rose | Sage | Deter aphis |
| Fruit trees | Garlic | Planted in a circle at the base of trees, garlic deters borers | Strawberry | Borage | Improves soil nutrition for strawberries |
| Grape | Clover | Increases soil fertility for grapes | Strawberry | Mustard | Helps control nematodes, improves soil |
| Grape | Hyssop | Vine crop increases | Strawberry | Marigold | Controls nematodes |
| Kohl Rabi | Borage | Reduces pests on kohl rabi | Tomato | Marigold | Improves growth and fruiting |
| Leek | Celery, onions | Leeks grow better | Tomato | Basil | Improves flavour and growth |

| Plant | Companion | Comments |
|-------|-----------|----------|
| Tomato | Thyme, peppermint | Help control white fly |
| Valerian | All vegetables | Adds vigour to vegetables |
| Yarrow | Medicinal herbs | Adds vigour to medicinal herbs and essential oils |

## Beneficial Plant Combinations

Bean with borage, larkspur, lovage, mustard, marjoram, rosemary, sage, anise, basil or savory.
Capsicum with basil.
Cabbage with celery, clover, hyssop, scented geranium, wormwood, basil, dill, mints, oregano, rosemary, sage or thyme.
Carrots with leeks, onions, rosemary, sage, wormwood, chervil, chives, garlic, parsley.
Corn with peanuts or beans.
Fruit trees with dandelion, garlic, nasturtium or mustard.
Lettuce with dill, feverfew or onion.
Most vegetables with tarragon.
Most scented herbs with yarrow.
Roses with corriander, garlic, marigold or tansy.
Strawberry with borage, marigold, onion or sage.
Tomato with basil, bee balm, chives, garlic, marigold, mint, sage, thyme, borage, lemon balm or parsley.
Peas with caraway.
Cucurbits with chamomile or oregano.
Onion with chamomile or dill.
Radishes with chervil.
Grape with chives.
Potatoes with coriander or tansy.

## Detrimental Plant Combinations

The following plants have a detrimental effect upon each other:

Beans with mugwort, beet, onions, garlic, fennel or chives.

Buttercup with legumes (e.g. peas, beans, clover, broom, etc).
Cherry trees near potatoes or wheat.
Cabbage or brussel sprouts with grapes, strawberries, beans, onions or rue.
Carrot with anise or dill.
Corn with onions or tomatoes.
Fennel with caraway, coriander, bean or pepper.
Gladioli with peas or beans.
Knotweed (i.e. *Polygonum*) inhibits growth in turnips.
Mugwort retards growth of many common garden plants (but deters many insects).
Narcissus seems to be badly affected by lily of the valley (Convallaria).
Onions with corn, cabbage, potatoes, sage or beans.
Potatoes with cherry trees, apricots, onions or rosemary.
Rue with basil, cabbage, sage or figs.
Sage with onion, rue or wormwood or cucumber.
Seeds under walnuts.
Strawberry with garlic.
Tomatoes with corn, beetroot, dill, fennel or apricots.
Walnut with vegetables, apples, azaleas, rhododendrons or lilacs. (Walnut root secretions poison most plants—daylilies are one exception).
Wormwood near compost (it repels earthworms).

It is worth noting that sometimes when two plants are grown together one does well, but the other does not. For example, when tomatoes and cabbages are grown together, the tomato benefits from the cabbage but the cabbage does not benefit from the tomato.

## Soil-improving Plants

**Alfalfa** Takes nitrogen from the air and adds it to the soil, increasing soil fertility. All legumes will do this, but alfalfa is more effective than most. It has very deep roots, reaching 10 m or more in depth, which bring nutrients from deep soils to the surface layers where they can be of benefit to other plants when the alfalfa dies and decomposes. Alfalfa grows particularly well with dandelions and is very beneficial when planted amongst grasses.

**Borage** An excellent cover crop for raising levels of potassium, calcium and some other minor nutrients.

**Caraway** Helps improve the subsoil if grown on wet clay soils.

**Dandelion** Roots up to 1 m deep help break the subsoil and raise nutrients (particularly calcium) to the upper soil layers. When the plant dies, the thick tap root is eaten out by worms and other creatures, allowing them to penetrate deeper into the soil.

**Black alder** Adds nitrogen to the soil in much the same way as legumes.

## Green Manure Crops

Green manure crops are crops that are allowed to grow for a period of time and then dug back into the ground to return nutrients to the soil and condition the soil with organic material.

### Nitrogen-fixing green manure crops

Alfalfa *Medicago sativa*

Black medic *Medicago lupilina*

Broad beans *Vicia faba*

Vetch *Vicia villosa*

Native sarsparilla *Hardenbergia* spp.

Clover *Trifolium* spp.

Cowpea *Vigna unguiculata*

Lupins *Lupinus angustifilius*

Chickpea *Civer arietinum*

### Non-nitrogen-fixing green manure crops

Annual ryegrass *Lolium multiflorum*

Comfrey *Symphytum x uplandicum*

Mustard *Sinapsis alba*

Borage *Borago officinalis*

Buckwheat *Fagopyrum esculentum*

Millet *Millium effusum*

Rye *Ecale cereale*

## Using Herbs to Control Pests

| Pest | Treatment |
|------|-----------|
| Ants | Plant peppermint or pennyroyal; sprinkle peppermint oil. |
| Aphis | Plant nasturtium-aphis are attracted to nasturtium if soil is acidic (liming soil may deter aphis from nasturtium). In a greenhouse, burn oak leaves to control aphis. |
| Cutworms | A mulch of oak leaves. |
| Dogs | Plant *Calendula officinalis*. Crush and spread leaves of *Coleus caninus*. |
| Fleas | Plant fennel or walnut trees. Spread walnut leaves around. |
| Flies | Plant basil or tansy. |
| Mice or rats | Peppermint oil or crushed leaves. Plant daffodils, grape hyacinths or scilla. |
| Mites | Plant garlic. |
| Moths | Spread dried lavender. |
| Mosquitoes | Plant basil, southernwood, peppermint or castor oil plant. |
| Nematodes | Spray or drench with a sugar solution (this can dehydrate the pest). High organic content in soils encourages fungi which attack plant parasitic types of nematodes. Plant marigolds, dahlias, asparagus or salvia to deter nematodes. |
| Rabbits | Cinerarias have been recorded as a repellant. |

## Organic Sprays

There are safe, environmentally-sound sprays which can be used in the garden. They may not have the 'bulldozer effect' of the more potent chemicals, but they are safe for both you and the environment, and if used properly will control most of your pest and disease problems.

When using organic sprays it is important to:
• Use the right spray for the right problem.
• Use the right strength.
• Spray thoroughly.
• Spray often, until the problem goes.

It pays to follow some basic rules with all sprays, even organic ones:
• Don't use cooking containers (e.g. saucepans) for making sprays.

- Clearly label your sprays and keep them out of children's reach.
- Protect your skin when spraying and avoid breathing the spray.
- Don't spray on hot or windy days.
- Only spray plants which need to be sprayed.

To make an organic herb spray:
1. Place 1 cup of herb leaves in 1 litre of boiling water.
2. Keep on the boil for a minute or two.
3. Allow the water to cool, then strain off the leaves.
4. Place the insect pest in a jar and spray it lightly with the herb spray.
5. If the pest dies, use this strength of spray. If it survives, double the amount of leaves used and make another test batch. Increase the amount of leaves until you achieve an effective strength.

*Note*: Some sprays are repellants and though they won't kill, they will make your 'test pest' extremely agitated.

Another, but less popular method, is to use the insect to make a repellant. The pest insect is crushed and mixed with water and sprayed onto the affected plants. This method is based on the theory that the smell of decaying insects will repel living insects of the same species.

## Soapy water spray

Soapy water sprays are effective against caterpillars, aphis, mealy bug and scale. It kills the insects by putting a film of soap over the insects' bodies. As such, the spray must contact and cover the insects to work properly. To make the spray mix 16 gm of pure soap powder with 2 litres of water.

## Quassia spray

Quassia spray kills most soft-bodied insects such as aphis, caterpillars and even leafhoppers, but does not kill insects with a hard shell such as ladybirds and beetles. It is made from wood chips of the plant *Picrasma quassioides.*

Boil 45 gm of quassia chips in water for 30 minutes. Strain the water while still warm and add 40 gm of soap flakes.

Mix one part of this solution with two parts of cold water.

## Garlic spray

Garlic spray helps control both insects and fungal diseases. It is particularly effective for controlling sucking insects such as mealy bugs and aphis, and on fungal problems usually treated with sulphur sprays.

Mix 120 gm of chopped garlic, 2 tablespoons of paraffin oil, 20 gm soap powder and 500 ml of water. Leave to stand for two days; strain, bottle and store in a dark, cool place. Add 1 part of this solution to 50 parts of water when ready to spray.

## Pyrethrum spray

This spray is made from the flower heads of either *Chrysanthemum cinerariaefolium* or *Chrysanthemum roseum.* It is effective against most insects.

Add 1 tablespoon of flower heads to 1 litre of hot water, allow to stand for 1 hour, then strain off the flower heads and add a pinch or two of soap powder. Mix and spray.

## Rhubarb spray

This spray is used to control aphis. Boil 1 kg of rhubarb leaves (not stems) in 2 litres of water for 30 minutes. Strain leaves and add the remaining water solution to 9 litres of water. Use within 24 hours. Do not eat plants within two days of spraying.

## Mustard dust

Grind mustard seed into a fine powder. Put into a jar with some nail holes punched in the lid. Shake over plants to control powdery mildew.

## Stinging nettle spray

Spray made from stinging nettle leaves (*Urtica urens*) is rich in iron and can be sprayed on plants as a nutrient fertiliser. The spray is also reported to help control pests and diseases.

Place chopped stinging nettle plants in a bucket of water, cover and allow to stand for three weeks, or until the foliage has rotted down. Strain off the remaining plant material to obtain the nettle liquid.

## Chamomile spray

Chamomile spray can be used as an insecticide spray, similar to pyrethrum. Bruised leaves also deter mosquitos and flies.

### White cedar spray

A spray made from the leaves of the white cedar (*Melia azederach*) repels grasshoppers. Steep the leaves in boiling water and cool before use.

### Eucalyptus spray

Sprays made from crushed leaves of eucalypts repels earwigs, slaters, ants and cockroaches. Applications should be done with care, as beneficial earthworms may be adversely affected.

### Other sprays

Here are some other simple sprays you can make yourself:

Mildew: spray milk every few days on affected plants.

Most insects: spray a thin mixture of flour and water directly onto the insect. This dries over the insect and suffocates it. A mixture of fine clay and water can be used the same way.

Nematodes: drench the affected soil with a sugar solution.

Slugs and snails: boil chopped wormwood leaves and spray the cooled solution every few days on affected areas.

## Plant Lures

Some plants can be used to attract insect and other pests away from treasured plants by using them as lures or decoys. Some examples are:

| Lures | Pests |
|---|---|
| Alfalfa (*Medicago sativa*) | bugs |
| Black nightshade (*Solanum nigrum*) | chewing beetles |
| Fat hen (*Chenopodium album*) | leafminers |
| Hyssop (*Hyssopus officinalis*) | cabbage white butterflies |
| Thorn apple (*Datura stamonium*) | chewing beetles |
| Mustard (*Brassica nigra*) | cabbage white butterflies |
| Nasturtium (*Tropaeolum majus*) | aphids |

# 4 Growing Herbs in Containers

Pots, tubs, baskets or any other type of container can be a great way to grow herbs. Container gardens offer more flexibility than growing in the ground. You can move your garden about, bringing plants to the foreground when they are at their best and hiding them when their appearance deteriorates. This is a particular advantage with many herbs which seasonally die back to the roots, leaving the pot bare.

Herbs grown in containers are ideal for people with limited space, and provide easy access for people who find ordinary gardening difficult. Kitchen herbs are particularly handy growing in a tub by the back door, or in pots on a kitchen window sill.

If your soil is poorly drained or infertile, container growing is one way to ensure good growing conditions. Large and invasive plants can be kept to a manageable size, and when conditions get too harsh the plant can be easily moved into a protected position.

## Caring for Herbs in Containers

### Watering

Pot plants dry out faster than those in the ground. Check the growing medium every few days (even more frequently in hot or windy weather) by feeling 2–3 cm below the surface. A drip irrigation system will ensure the pots do not dry out. Another solution is to use larger containers which are less likely to dry out. A third method is to stand the pots on moist carpet underfelt—the plant roots will soak up the moisture.

Overly-dry soil can be difficult to re-wet. If this happens, immerse the pot for a few minutes in a bucket or tub full of water. Leave it there until the air bubbles stop rising from the container.

### Feeding

Potted herbs should be fed regularly because nutrients are washed through the soil. Use slow release fertilisers two to three times a year and regularly apply a liquid fertiliser such as Maxicrop or Aquasol during the active growing season.

### Pruning and harvesting

Most herbs withstand ruthless pruning, in fact the best growth for cooking is lush young foliage which sprouts after a hard prune. However, this lush growth is susceptible to wind, heat and cold, so move your pots into a protected place immediately after pruning.

### Potting up

After a year or two, most potted herbs start to become pot bound (i.e. there are too many roots in the pot) and repotting is necessary. Plants can be put back in the same pot if you remove some of the top growth and cut away some of the old roots. This allows you to add fresh, fertile soil. Alternatively pot up into a larger container.

## Ventilation and temperature

Most herbs prefer temperatures between 10 and 30° C. Fresh air is also important, particularly in humid climates. Space the pots about 10–15 cm apart so air can circulate, and problems with disease will be greatly reduced.

## Maintenance

Unfortunately container-grown herbs can lose their form easily. In a kitchen garden, constant cutting to use pieces will keep plants compact and in shape. However, never remove more than one-fifth of the plant's foliage at any one time.

Hanging baskets can dry out very easily in warm or windy weather. They are best placed on the ground in shady protected areas in warmer weather.

All types of containers should be turned every few weeks so that every side of the plant receives light.

# Choosing the Right Container

A good container is one which drains well, looks good, doesn't break and holds enough soil to support the plant. Be careful of medium-sized or large glazed ceramic pots with only one hole in the bottom: these will not provide sufficient drainage for most herbs. Wood containers look good, but unless treated with timber preservative (e.g. painted inside with bitumen), they can rot.

Many herbs grow well in hanging baskets, provided they are kept well watered. A basket plant will always dry out faster than a pot plant on the ground.

A large container can be planted with several different herbs, providing you choose plants with similar vigour (i.e. if you mix strong-growing plants with weaker-growing ones, the weaker plants will be choked out).

Breather bags can also be used for growing herbs. These are woven polypropylene bags which are porous yet stable, allowing plant roots to grow evenly throughout the media. Roots do not become pot bound so plants can be kept in breather bags for up to four years.

# Potting Mixes

A good potting mix is free of diseases and weed seeds, and has a very even texture. Avoid mixes which have lumps of clay, stones or odd-sized chunks

## Types of Containers - At a Glance

| Type | Weight | Cost | Drainage | Use | Problems |
|------|--------|------|----------|-----|----------|
| Terracotta (unglazed) | Heavy | High | Very good | Excellent for plants needing very good drainage. | Can become too dry in hot weather. |
| Ceramic (glazed) | Heavy | High | Average | Good for indoors or displays. | May have insufficient drainage holes. |
| Plastic | Light | Low | Average | Varies according to type. | Some types are brittle, especially after lengthy exposure to light. |
| Timber | Average | Medium to average | Average | Decorative | Some woods rot and may require treatment with preservative. |
| Wire basket | Light | Low | Very good | Hanging from eaves, on verandahs, etc. | Exposure to wind can cause drying out. |
| Plastic basket | Light | Low | Good | As above for wire basket. | Doesn't dry as fast as wire basket. |

of bark or compost. Good mixes cost more, but will keep the plants much healthier. The Standards Association of Australia has set non-compulsory standards for potting mixes. A mix which is endorsed by the association is preferable.

If you want to make up your own mix, use only the best ingredients. A good general mix is 2 parts sieved, well-rotted compost from your compost heap, 1 part coarse washed river sand and 1 part sandy loam. Avoid soils with shells or lumps of white chalk, and sands and soils that are likely to have high salt levels (e.g. beach sand).

## Herbs For Pots

Herbs For Small and Medium-sized Pots
*Aloe vera*, basil, calendula, five-seasons herb (*Coleus amboinicus*), lemon balm, marjoram, mint, oregano, parsley and thyme.

### Herbs for Large Pots and Tubs

*Aloe vera*, bay laurel, citrus, cloves, coffee, lavender (Canary Island or Italian), lemon grass, lemon-scented tea tree, lemon verbena, scented pelargoniums, southernwood, rose, rosemary, sage and wormwood.

### Herbs for Hanging Baskets

Alpine strawberry, *Ajuga reptans*, calendula, chamomile, pennyroyal mint, golden marjoram, nasturtium, creeping rosemary and thyme.

## Herbs as Indoor Plants

Many herbs can be grown indoors. Small-growing herbs can be placed on a window sill or kitchen bench where they receive plenty of light and are in easy reach when you are cooking. You can grow several different herbs in the one container, although it is perhaps better to keep them segregated so that no one herb competes too strongly with the others. Larger herbs can be grown in larger containers, perhaps being used not only to harvest, but also for indoor decoration, and to add a pleasant scent to the air as people brush past.

Remember though, that conditions are not always ideal inside. Most herbs will grow happily in rooms that are a little too cool for human comfort, and often room temperatures will be too high, especially if the house is heated or the plants are placed near cooking appliances. If you are growing herbs in heated rooms you will need to create a moist microclimate around the plant. This can be achieved by the following methods:

1. Misting—Use a fine spray to cover the foliage with small droplets of water. Misting lowers soil and plant temperatures, overcomes moisture loss, and discourages red spider mite. Do not mist plants in the evening or when plants are exposed to bright sunlight.

2. Group all pot plants together—Air trapped in the foliage will increase the relative humidity.

3. Double potting—Use an outer waterproof container and fill the space between the pot and container with moist peat. Double potting provides a moisture reservoir below the pot and also insulates the compost.

Indoor light levels can be too low for some herbs. In temperate climates most plants need direct sun in winter for at least three to four hours every day. In warmer climates direct sun, even in winter, may scorch the plant and dry out the soil. Plants should be taken outside at intervals to build up carbohydrate levels which are essential for growth. This should be done in temperate seasons when temperatures are not going to be at extreme levels.

### Herbs to Grow Indoors

#### In cool climates

| As a kitchen window garden | In a large container |
| --- | --- |
|  | Bay laurel |
| Chervil | *Coleus caninus* |
| Chives | Madder |
| Coriander | Lavender |
| Dill | Lemon grass |
| Hyssop | Scented geraniums |

*As a kitchen window garden*

Lemon balm
Mint—most types
Marigold
Mustard
Nettle
Oregano
Parsley
Peppermint
Rosemary
Rue
Sage
Salad burnet
Savory
Sorrel
Tarragon
Thyme
Valerian
Wallflower

*In a large container*

Tansy
Pennyroyal
Yarrow

**In warm climates**

*As a kitchen window garden*

Chives
Coriander
Ginger
Oregano
Parsley
Sage
Tumeric
Sweet marjoram
Fenugreek

*In a large container*

Camphor laurel
*Coleus caninus*
Lemon verbena
Lemon grass
Pineapple sage

# 5 Using Herbs

## Harvesting herbs

Foliage, flowers, fruit, seed, bark, and even roots, rhizomes and bulbs are harvested from herb plants. With all plant parts it is critical to harvest at the right time. The oils and other chemicals which make a herb valuable, in most cases, are at their best at only one stage of the plant's growth. Medicinal herbs in particular can lose much of their value if harvested too early or late.

No matter what part of the plant you harvest, the procedure is usually the same:

1. Harvest in cool weather.
2. Cut off the required parts with clean, sharp tools.
3. Remove as much unwanted material (soil, insects, etc.) as possible while still outside.
4. Clean the plant material as soon as possible, removing damaged, dead or marked tissue and any foreign material including insects and soil. Avoid washing the plant—this may remove oils.
5. Process the material as soon as possible (distillation, drying, etc) to minimise loss of oils or other chemicals.

## Handling freshly picked herbs

Once picked, most fresh herbs will rapidly wilt and lose colour, essential oils and other aromatic compounds. This deterioration can be slowed in a number of ways:

• Herbs grown under optimum temperature and soil moisture conditions do not deteriorate as quickly as herbs grown in poor conditions. In other words, the healthier and more vigorous the plant is when harvested, the longer it will last.

• Deterioration will be slower if plants are harvested when the aromatic compounds and oils are at optimum levels. In some plants, including rosemary and sage, this is just before flowering; for other plants the optimum harvest time may be at a different stage of the plant's growth.

• Most fresh herbs are best stored at a refrigerator temperature of around 1° C. A few herbs—for example, watercress and basil—are sensitive to chilling and should not be stored at low temperatures (a temperature around 5 to 6° C would be preferable). A 10° C reduction in the temperature of the harvested herb will generally increase its storage life by three to four times. Harvesting your herbs in the coolest part of the morning will also help get them down to storage temperature more quickly. Do not store at temperatures below 1° C as freezing will damage plant tissue.

• Water loss is reduced if high humidity is maintained around the fresh herb. Plastic film wraps are ideal although you must make breather holes in the plastic to prevent condensation forming on the plant tissue.

• Fresh herbs are often very soft and easily damaged during harvesting. Mint, basil and coriander are particularly susceptible to bruising which makes them more prone to moisture loss, discolouring and microbial infection. Careful handling during harvest will prolong their storage life.

# Drying herbs

Anyone can dry herbs. All you need is a cool and well-ventilated room. Your harvested plants are simply tied in bunches and hung upside down from the roof or curtain rods. Don't do this in a room which will steam up (i.e. avoid kitchens and bathrooms), and try to find a relatively dark place—direct sunlight can reduce oil content.

In humid climates, drying bunches may develop fungal growths. To prevent this problem use a well-ventilated room (a fan may be helpful) and keep the bunches small and well-spaced to allow air to move between bunches.

After drying, foliage can be stripped and either used immediately or stored in sealed, dry containers. Roots (and sometimes other parts) are often ground into a powder after drying. Containers should be labelled with the name of the plant and the time of harvesting.

# Cooking with herbs

Herbs are not foods in the strict sense of the word, but they do provide essential nutrients in the diet, not to mention the flavour they add to many foods. Bland and unattractive food can be made far more interesting with the addition of herbs.

It is important to use herbs correctly. While they are an easy way to enhance the flavour of a dish, they can just as easily ruin a preparation if used incorrectly.
• Too much of a herb can overshadow the natural flavour of the food it is added to.
• Too little of a herb in a dish will achieve nothing.
• The addition of herbs must be balanced to complement other flavours in the dish.
• It is important to blend different herbs in appropriate ratios to achieve the best results.

The flavour imparted to food by a herb depends on:
1. The stage of growth and time of year the herb was harvested.
2. The part of the plant which is used.
3. The length of time the herb is left to stand in liquid or solid mixtures before it is used.
4. The temperature of the dish.
5. The moisture content of the dish which is being cooked (e.g. A stew will absorb flavours differently to a piece of barbecued meat).

## Herb vinegars

Herb vinegar is made by placing fresh herbs in a bottle of vinegar and letting it stand, sealed, for at least two to three weeks. The flavour will disperse from the herbs more readily if the bottles are stood in the sun. Herb vinegars are ideal as salad dressings, or used in the same way as normal vinegar in cooking. Suitable herbs include tarragon, sage, marjoram, thyme and savory.

## Herb oils

Herb oils are made in much the same way as herb vinegars. The herbs are placed in non-aromatic oils such as safflower or sunflower oil and allowed to stand a couple of weeks before use. Herb oils can be used for cooking or in salads to give flavour to food.

## Herb cheese

To make herb cheese melt grated cheese in a saucepan, add chopped herbs and pour the mixture into moulds. Allow to cool then store by wrapping in foil.

Try this 200-year-old recipe from Cumberland, England:
*110 g grated cheese*
*2 tablespoons thickened cream*
*3 teaspoons sherry*
*2 tablespoons of a mix of chopped parsley, sage, thyme, tarragon, chives, chervil and winter savory*

Stir over gentle heat in a saucepan, then pour into moulds. Serve cold.

## Herb salt

Place alternate thin layers of salt and roughly chopped fresh herbs in a jar. Seal and store for several weeks before removing herbs with a sieve. The salt will retain the flavour of the herbs.

## Herb honey

Add finely chopped herbs to honey and mix thoroughly before storing in a sealed jar. The mixture should be left to stand for several weeks before using. Try the following combinations:

Parsley and honey—Add to cooked carrots.
Marjoram, thyme and honey—Use as a salad dressing.

## Herb confectionery

Toffees, coconut ice and other home-made sweets can be flavoured by placing a layer of chopped herbs on the bottom of the container into which the candy mixture is poured. Suitable herbs include mints (most varieties) and scented geraniums.

## Herb biscuits

Standard biscuit recipes can be flavoured with herbs. It is important to choose herbs which are compatible with sweet flavours though! These include spearmint, lime-scented geranium, pineapple sage and peppermint geranium. Do not use savoury herbs like marjoram or savory in biscuits.

## Herb mustards

These are made by mixing chopped herb leaves or crushed seeds with plain mustard. Plain mustard can be made by mixing mustard flour (ground mustard seed) with a good quality cream, a pinch of salt and a couple of drops of tarragon vinegar. Add parsley, tarragon, chives or chervil to the mustard and leave it to stand for a week or two before using. (Use 2 tablespoons of herbs to ½ litre of mustard.)

## Herb teas

Herb teas have been consumed for thousands of years in all parts of the world. A herb tea is made by mixing boiling water with a herb to extract the flavour or essence of the herb into the hot water. Herb teas can be drunk hot or cold, using fresh or dried herbs.

Herb teas can be made from a mixture of different types of herbs and may be used for medicinal or purely culinary purposes.

Serving the tea the correct way is, in some places, considered an art in itself. The flavour of a tea can vary according to:
• Whether the teapot is warm or cold.
• How long the tea is left to draw before serving.
• How quickly the tea is drunk after serving.
• How much herb material is used in the pot.
• The stage of growth of the herb material when it is harvested.
• The quality of water used.
• Whether the herb material is fresh or dried.

Tea connoisseurs usually follow the rules below:
• Warm the teapot first.
• One teaspoon of tea per person and one for the pot.
• Stand for 3 minutes before serving.
• Use fresh unchlorinated water.
• Never use milk as this can affect the pure flavour of the tea.

## Common herb teas

**Lemon balm tea**  A very old, traditional tea from Europe. A little rosemary, spearmint, lavender or clove may be added for extra flavour.
**Bergamot tea**  Was used by the American Indians and early colonists. Bergamot is used to flavour Earl Grey tea.
**Chamomile tea**  One of the most popular teas in the world for centuries. It is made from the flowers of chamomile and is drunk hot or cold. Many people like to sweeten their tea with honey or orange. For something different add fennel seed (2 parts chamomile flowers to 1 part fennel seed) or a small quantity of grated ginger to the steeping brew.
**Lemon verbena tea**  Use 5 or 6 leaves per teacup. Drink hot or cold.
**Peppermint tea**  May be served as straight peppermint tea, or flavoured by adding honey, alfalfa, clover flowers or linden flowers.
**Rosemary tea**  Was recommended centuries ago by Arabian physicians. Lemon, honey or a few lavender flowers may be added for extra flavour.

# Using Herbs With Fruit

Herbs can enhance and add flavour to a wide variety of fruit desserts including stewed fruit, dessert pies, cakes, souffles and ice-creams, to mention only a few possibilities.

The following combinations work well:

**Angelica**  Add chopped leaves to fruit salads; use candied stems as a garnish.

**Bay leaf**  Add a leaf to baked custard.

**Bergamot**  Add chopped leaves to flavour stewed apricots, peaches, plums, apples, pears and berries.

**Borage**  Use candied flowers as a garnish on any dessert.

**Scented geranium**  Add chopped leaves to cakes and dessert pies; use leaves or flowers as a garnish.

**Lavender**  Add flowers to dishes with raspberries, blueberries, blackberries and currants and to sauces, custard and ice-cream.

**Lemon balm**  Add chopped leaves to fruit salads and sorbets; add leaves to cakes and pies for lemon flavouring.

**Mint**  Add leaves to fresh fruit salad, pies, cakes, sorbets, ice-creams and sauces.

**Rosemary**  Should only be used with strong tasting fruits such as citrus.

**Sage**  Add small quantities to stewed apples or pears (too much spoils the taste).

**Sweet woodruff**  Leaves are traditionally used with strawberries and rhubarb; use flowers as a garnish on desserts.

**Thyme**  Add small quantities to enhance the flavour of stewed apples and apple pies.


## Herb Recipes

### Baked Red Cabbage

| | |
|---|---|
| *1 small red cabbage* | *salt, pepper and crushed* |
| *1 large onion* | *dill seeds to taste* |
| *3 large cooking apples* | *cooking oil* |
| | *water* |

Chop cabbage and onions; peel, core and slice apples, and arrange these ingredients in layers in a baking dish or tray. Sprinkle salt, pepper and dill. Pour over a little oil and water. Bake at 180° C for 20 minutes.

### Gingernut Biscuits

| | |
|---|---|
| *110 g butter* | *1 cup plain flour* |
| *1 cup sugar* | *2 teaspoons baking* |
| *1 tablespoon golden* | *powder* |
| *syrup* | *2 teaspoons ground* |
| *1 egg, beaten* | *ginger* |

Melt butter, sugar and golden syrup in a saucepan over low heat. Allow to cool before adding remaining ingredients. Mix well, roll into small balls and place on a greased tray. Press each ball with the back of a fork to flatten. Bake at 180° C until golden brown.

### Fast Mint Sauce

| | |
|---|---|
| *1 cup mint leaves* | *small pinch of salt* |
| *1 dessertspoon finely* | *juice from half a lemon* |
| *chopped onion* | *2 teaspoons honey* |

Mix all ingredients to a paste in a blender, or grind them with a pestle and mortar. Add water to thin the paste as required.

### Dandelion Coffee

Gather dandelion roots in autumn. Wash the roots thoroughly, but do not cut them. Bake the whole roots in a moderate oven until they turn a deep brown colour. Allow them to cool then grind into a fine powder which can be used as a coffee substitute.

### Mint Pasty (a traditional recipe from Northern England)

| | |
|---|---|
| *2 cups finely chopped* | *2 cups brown sugar* |
| *mint* | *pastry* |
| *2 cups currants* | |

Mix currants, mint and sugar. Add sufficient water so that the mixture can be rolled into a cylinder which holds together without crumbling. Wrap the cylinder in pastry sheets and bake in moderate oven until the pastry turns a golden brown colour. Baking time and temperature will depend on the size of the pasty—for your first batch try 12 minutes at 200° C.

### Herb Dip

| | |
|---|---|
| *200 gm container plain* | *1 tablespoon celery seed* |
| *low fat yogurt* | *1 tablespoon chopped* |
| *1 tablespoon chopped* | *capsicum* |
| *parsley* | *1 tablespoon dried* |
| *1 tablespoon chopped* | *onion powder* |
| *chives* | |

Mix all ingredients, stand for one hour and serve with sticks of celery and carrot as an appetizer.

### Mixed Herb Barbecue Marinade

| | |
|---|---|
| *1/4 cup olive oil* | *1 tablespoon chopped* |
| *3 cloves* | *chives or shallots* |
| *2 tablespoons chopped* | *1 tablespoon chopped* |
| *parsley* | *rosemary or tarragon* |

| 1 tablespoon chopped | 2 sprigs lemon thyme or |
| basil | lemon verbena |

Mix all ingredients in a food processor, then pour over meat. Stand for half an hour to several hours before cooking. Pour marinade over the meat as it cooks.

## Corn soup (serves six)

| 2 cloves garlic, minced | 1/4 cup grated carrot |
| 1/2 cup chopped parsley | 1/4 cup chopped celery |
| 2 cups fresh or frozen | 1/2 teaspoon diced |
| corn kernels | capsicum |
| 3 cups chicken soup | 1 cup milk |
| 1/2 cup chopped onions | |

Mix all ingredients, except milk, in a saucepan as you bring them to the boil. Once boiling, reduce heat and simmer for 10 minutes. Allow to cool and puree in a blender. Strain through a standard sieve and return to saucepan with the milk. Simmer for 5 minutes and serve.

Hint: Pour a tablespoon of cream on top of each bowl of soup after serving.

# Herb Breads

(written by staff at the Bread Research Institute, Sydney)

Many herbs have distinctive flavours which are ideal for flavouring bread, either mixed with butter and spread on baked bread, or mixed in the dough before baking.

Herb breads are not difficult to make. Recipes which use yeast will take time to prepare, but many recipes can be made using self-raising flour. Breads made in this way have a different texture to yeast bread and may become stale faster, but there will rarely be any left at the end of the day anyway. Left-overs freeze well and can be reheated in a microwave oven.

Experimenting with different herbs in bread can be great fun. There are no fixed rules, so if you feel that a particular herb or mixture of herbs might go well with bread, try it. If you are not so sure of your baking skills, try one of the following recipes which have been developed by the Bread Research Institute of Australia. These recipes have been thoroughly tested and are sure to produce a great result.

*Note:* Fresh or dried herbs can be used in all recipes. When fresh herbs are out of season substitute 1 teaspoon of dried herb for 1 tablespoon of fresh herbs.

## Herb and Garlic Bread Sticks (makes a baker's dozen)

| 2 cups wholemeal or | 2/3 cup milk |
| white flour | 2 tablespoons melted |
| 2 teaspoons mixed dried | butter |
| herbs of your choice | 1/2 teaspoon crushed |
| cracked black pepper | garlic |
| 1 egg | sesame seeds |

Combine flour, herbs and pepper. Beat egg with milk, add to dry ingredients and mix to form a soft dough. Knead lightly on a floured board until smooth. Roll out to a rectangle 24 cm x 15 cm and cut into 13 even-sized strips. Melt butter in a lamington pan, stir in garlic. Roll dough strips in the melted butter and arrange in a row down the centre of the pan. Sprinkle with sesame seeds. Bake 10–15 minutes in a hot oven. Serve with soups or salad.

## Thyme and Pumpkin Damper

| 3 cups white self-raising | 1 tablespoon chopped |
| flour | Italian parsley |
| 1 cup barley bran | 2 1/2 cups grated but- |
| 3 teaspoons dried thyme | ternut pumpkin* |
| leaves, torn | 1 1/2 cups water or |
| 1 teaspoon sugar | milk |
| 1 teaspoon salt | 1/2 cup olive oil |

*Use ripe deep orange pumpkin

Stir dry ingredients together including herbs. Stir in pumpkin, olive oil and milk and mix to a soft dough. Knead gently on a lightly floured surface until smooth. Form into a damper shape, place in a well-greased deep 20 cm cake pan covered with an inverted tray or casserole dish lid. Bake for 1 hour at 220° C.

## Scandinavian-style Crispbread (makes 48)

| 1 1/2 cups wholemeal | 1/2 teaspoon dry |
| self-raising flour | mustard |
| 1 cup plain rye flour | 1 tablespoon dill seeds |
| 2 tablespoons raw sugar | 1/2 cup margarine |
| 1 teaspoon baking | 1/2 cup iced water |
| powder | 1 egg white |
| 1 teaspoon salt | sesame seeds |

Mix flours, sugar, baking powder, salt, mustard and dill seeds. Cut in margarine until coarse crumbs form. Sprinkle iced water and mix to a stiff dough. Knead lightly on a floured surface then divide dough into three pieces. Roll out each piece to a rectangle 30 x 25 cm on a floured surface, transfer to greased oven trays and cut into 16 even-sized rectangles (2.5 cm x 5 cm). Prick well with a fork, brush with egg white and sprinkle with sesame seeds. Bake in a moderate oven at 180° C until browned (10–12 minutes). Cool on a rack.

## Savoury Luncheon Twist

| | |
|---|---|
| *3 cups plain flour* | *1 small onion, finely* |
| *1 teaspoon salt* | *chopped* |
| *1 teaspoon dried* | *1 clove garlic, crushed* |
| *tarragon* | *3 tablespoons extra* |
| *1/3 cup chopped parsley* | *butter* |
| *1 1/2 cups (185 g)* | *1 teaspoon prepared* |
| *grated Edam cheese* | *mustard* |
| *3/4 cup milk* | *1 ham steak, finely* |
| *2 tablespoons butter* | *chopped* |
| *20 g compressed yeast* | *freshly ground black* |
| *1 egg, lightly beaten* | *pepper* |

Mix flour, salt, tarragon, parsley and 1/2 cup of cheese in a bowl. Scald milk, add butter and cool to lukewarm. Stir in yeast and egg. Add liquid to dry ingredients and mix to form a firm dough. Knead well until smooth and elastic. Cover and set aside to rest for 20–30 minutes.

Saute onion and garlic in butter until limp. Add mustard and stir well. Roll dough out to a 50 x 25 cm rectangle, spread with onion mixture, sprinkle with remaining cheese and the ham. Roll up the dough Swiss roll style, and seal the edges. With a very sharp knife cut the roll into two lengthwise, making two 50 cm long pieces with the cut sides up. Moisten one end of each portion, press together to seal and twist the two pieces together by lifting one portion of the dough over the other, keeping the cut edges up. Shape into a ring, seal the ends, and place on a greased oven tray.

Proof until the dough is nearly doubled in size (approximately 35–45 minutes). Bake in a moderate oven for 20–30 minutes or until golden brown. Remove from oven, brush lightly with milk and return to the oven for 5 minutes. Serve warm with a crisp green salad.

Reference: *The Australian Breadmaking Handbook*

by staff at the Bread Research Institute, Epping Rd, North Ryde, Sydney.

## Herb Butters

These are easily made by adding chopped herbs to butter or margarine. They can be used as spreads on bread or melted over hot vegetables. Try these popular recipes:

### Maitre d'Hotel Butter

| | |
|---|---|
| *lemon juice* | *parsley, finely chopped* |
| *15 g butter* | *chervil, finely chopped* |

Add a few drops of lemon juice to the butter. Add herbs, beat into a cream and serve in squares on top of steaks.

### Green Butter

| | |
|---|---|
| *30 g butter* | *1 sprig watercress* |
| *1/4 clove garlic, crushed* | *1 sprig chervil* |
| *1 shallot* | *cayenne powder* |
| *salt* | |

Rub all ingredients through a fine sieve and store in the fridge.

# Home Herbal Remedies

*Note:* The following information is not intended to replace the services of a physician or naturopath. You should always consult a professional to treat serious ailments.

Herbs have been used for medicinal purposes for over 5000 years. Modern herbalism, however, had its beginnings with the ancient Greeks around 1000 BC. Hippocrates—often called the father of medicine—and a number of other Greek intellectuals made a thorough scientific study of medicinal herbs Through experimentation and observation they determined the medicinal characteristics of a large proportion of the medicinal herbs we use today. Their findings were passed down through Western civilisation over the next 3000 years.

During the 19th century and early part of the 20th

Wood betony

Pot marigold (*Calendula officinalis*)

Caraway (*Carum carvi*)

Cardamon (*Elettaria cardamomum*)

Catnip (*Nepeta cataria*)

Roman chamomile (*Anthemis nobilis*)

Greater celandine (*Chelidonium majus*)

Chervil (*Anthriscus cerefolium*)

Chicory (*Chichorium intybus*)

Chives, rosemary and thyme
in a terracotta herb pot.

Garlic chives (*Allium tuberosum*)

Sweet cicely (*Myrrhis odorata*)

Cinnamon (*Cinnamomum zeylanicum*)

century, there was a major turning away from traditional herbal medicine in some parts of the Western world, including Australia, as people embraced the new ways of modern science. The doctor largely replaced the naturopath and herbalist. In recent years, however, there has been a re-emergence of traditional medicine, bringing a more balanced approach to health care.

One of the major advantages of herbal medicines is that they lack the side effects of modern drugs. How often have you thought twice about taking a pain killer or allergy treatment because it makes you drowsy?

## Types of Herbal Medicines

**Alternatives**  Act to purify the blood and balance glandular functions, e.g. red clover flowers.

**Astringents**  Cause the skin or mucous membrane to become more tight or firm. They can be used as a wash or lotion on the skin or as a mouth wash. Mild astringents include foliage from rue and petals from Rosa gallica (rose). Stronger astringents include agrimony and sage.

**Bitter tonics**  Stimulate the flow of digestive juices and help cure a loss of appetite, e.g. dandelion root, hop flowers and chamomile flowers.

**Carminatives**  Reduce the formation of gas in the digestive system and promote the expulsion of gas, e.g. angelica seed, caraway seed, eucalyptus leaves and peppermint.

**Cathartics**  Cause the bowels to loosen. There are two types of cathartics: laxatives which have a mild action and purgatives which have a dramatic action. (NB: Cathartics should only be used occasionally.)

**Demulcants**  Reduce irritation in the digestive tract. They are normally bland liquids of a thick consistency which put a soothing and protective coating over mouth tissue and the digestive tract, e.g. comfrey root, licorice root.

**Diuretics**  Cause increased urinary secretions and help eliminate toxic substances from the body, e.g. parsley roots.

**Emollients**  Soothe and soften the skin, e.g. comfrey root, oatmeal and quince seeds.

**Expectorants**  Help loosen and expel phlegm in the lungs or respiratory tract, e.g. balm of Gilead buds, comfrey root, elecampane root, mullein and licorice.

**Nervines/Relaxants**  Cause a relaxation of the nervous system, calming a person with nervous irritation caused by strain, tiredness or excitement, e.g. chamomile tea and valerian root.

**Stimulants**  Help stimulate and regenerate the circulatory system. They do not act in the presence of excess animal foods (i.e. do not use after eating meat, cheese, etc) or alcohol, e.g. mustard, cinnamon, cloves, nutmeg, pennyroyal, peppermint, summer savory and vervain.

## Herbal baths

A long hot bath is one of the best ways to relax after a period of tension or hard work. Adding herbs (fresh leaves, bath salts or herb waters) can considerably improve the soothing effect of a bath.

### How to Prepare a Herb Bath

1. Place a handful of fresh herbs in a nylon stocking or tied in a muslin cloth.
2. Put the herb bag in the bottom of the bath and run very hot water over it for a couple of minutes (do not use cold water). (Alternatively soak the bag in a bucket filled with boiling water for 5 minutes and then add the water to the bath.)
3. Now run the bath with cold water as well as hot to bring it to the required depth and temperature.

To rejuvenate the skin add a mixture of comfrey, alfalfa, parsley and orange peel to the bath. For aching muscles add a mixture of chamomile and sage leaves.

## Treating Common Ailments

| Ailment | Herb | Method of Use |
| --- | --- | --- |
| Acne | Lemon grass | Drink the tea or use in a hot bath |
| Acne | Carrot | Drink the juice |
| Appetite (lack of) | Peppermint | Drink the tea |
| Arthritis | Feverfew | Eat a few leaves daily |
| Arthritis | Rosemary or lavender | Use in a herb bath |
| Asthma | Horseradish | Tablets |
| Asthma | Peppermint | Drink the tea |
| Asthma | Pine needles or lavender | In a hot bath |

| Ailment | Herb | Method of Use |
|---------|------|---------------|
| Common Cold | Garlic | Tablets for prevention |
| Common Cold | Pine needles | In a hot bath |
| Common Cold | Roman wormwood | Tonic |
| Cuts and abrasions | Calendula | Ointment on small wounds |
| Depression | Balm or oat straw | Drink the tea |
| Depression | Lavender | In a hot bath |
| Dermatitis | Lemon grass | In a hot bath |
| Insomnia | Valerian or Chamomile | Drink the tea |
| Gastritis | Peppermint | Drink the tea |
| Haemorrhoids | Pilewort or Witch hazel | Tablets |
| Headaches (tension) | Chamomile, thyme or rosemary | Drink the tea |
| Nausea | Rasberry leaf or spearmint | Drink the tea |
| Respiratory Problems | Garlic | Tablets |
| | Eucalyptus | Inhale the oil |
| | Peppermint | Inhale the oil |
| Sinusitis | Horseradish | Tablets |
| Sinusitis | Fenugreek | Drink the tea |

(*NB*: Some of these treatments will take months of constant use before giving significant results.)

## Gargles

Regular use of a gargle can stop bacterial growth in the mouth and strengthen the gums. Here are a few tried and proven recipes for gargles you can make yourself:

### Ginger Tea

Boil ginger root in water to make a lightly coloured tea. Add a little lemon juice and honey to remove the bitterness.

### Mint-Thyme Gargle

*2 cups ethyl alcohol
(75% proof)
1 teaspoon chopped
mint leaves
1 teaspoon chopped
thyme leaves*

*6 cloves
1 teaspoon grated
nutmeg
10 drops peppermint oil*

Mix all ingredients, except peppermint oil. Stand for 3 days. Strain off the herbs, add peppermint oil and shake well before using.

### Sage-Rosemary Gargle

*5 teaspoons chopped
sage leaves
5 teaspoons chopped
rosemary leaves*

*1 teaspoon cloves
1 teaspoon grated
ginger*

Mix all ingredients and boil in 1 litre of water for 5 minutes. Allow to cool and mix in a teaspoon of salt before using.

### Sage Tea

Gently boil 1/2 litre of water with 1 cup of sage leaves for 30 minutes. Allow to stand for another 30 minutes then strain off the leaves. Add enough cider vinegar to give the tea an acidic smell then mix in 2 teaspoons of honey to sweeten.

### Toothache

Try these herbal treatments for temporary relief from toothache:
• Oil of cloves put on a cotton bud and touched on the sore tooth.
• Chewing oregano leaves or ginger root may give relief.

### Hiccups

• Soak a small lump of sugar with 2–3 drops of peppermint oil, then chew.
• Drink peppermint tea (this is a milder cure).

# Herb Crafts

## Herb Dyes

Herb dyes can be used to colour clothing, tablecloths, scarves, curtains and any other items made from cloth or yarn. For some people this is a fascinating art form, for others it's a further way to use their herbs.

The process normally involves three steps:
1. Preparing the dye
The herb is soaked or boiled in water. The plant

tissue is then strained to produce a clean liquid dye.

2. Dyeing the cloth or yarn

The material is dipped or soaked in the dye—the length of time depends on the type of dye used and the effect required.

3. Mordanting

This involves treating the material with a mordant which stops the dye from washing out later on. Common mordants include alum, cream of tartar and tartaric acid. Potassium dichromate and copper sulphate can be used as mordants, but they will change the colour of the dye.

*Note*: stages 2 and 3 are sometimes combined (i.e. the mordant may be mixed with the dye solution in step 2).

Many herb dyes give natural, subtle tones, others can be very bright, although they are rarely harsh or garish. No matter what combination you use, the colours always seem to naturally blend together.

As with any type of dye, some herb dyes will fade over time. The reds and yellows tend to be more resistant to fading—some dyes have lasted for hundreds of years. Plants which lose their colour when boiled can be fermented instead: mash the plant and stand in water for a week or two before using.

## Red Dye

Madder root has been traditionally used to give a deep red colour to oriental rugs. After three years of growth, the madder roots are dug up, cleaned, dried and ground. About 200 g of powdered roots are soaked in water overnight, then boiled and immediately strained through gauze to extract the dyed water. Alum is used as a mordant to fix the brightness in reds.

Other red dyes can be obtained from dock, hops, lady's bedstraw, pokeweed, St John's Wort and sweet woodruff.

## Yellow Dye

Yellow dye can be obtained from the flowers of weld, safflower, agrimony, St John's wort, saffron, sunflower, dandelion and tansy.

## Blue Dye

Indigo is the most common source of blue dye and is made by fermenting the leaves. Flowers from woad, elder and elecampane are also used to create blue dyes.

## Black Dye

Black dyes can be extracted from alder, black walnut and woad.

## Purple Dye

Blackberry fruit, geranium, grapes (fruits) and lady's bedstraw will give purple dyes.

## Pressing Herbs

Plants can be preserved for hundreds of years by a simple technique known as 'pressing'. Pressed herbs can be used in many different ways—as a framed picture, stuck at the top of note paper, a scented greeting card, or even (for strong sprigs or large single leaves) as a scented bookmark. There are many ways of pressing plants (see below), although they all follow the same basic procedure:

1. The plant specimen is laid out flat on a sheet of absorbent material, e.g. newspaper.
2. A second sheet is placed on top of the plant.
3. The sheets are then placed in a situation where pressure can be applied to squeeze all the liquid from the plant tissue. Sheets used to dry plants with soft, moist tissues will need to be changed regularly—particularly in the first few days of pressing.
4. After a period of time—anything from a week to several months—the plant can be removed and mounted on a sheet of paper or card.
5. The mounted specimen should be stored in a dry situation to enhance preservation.

### Ways to press herbs

1. Plant press   A plant press consists of two wooden boards (approximately 40 cm x 30 cm) which are clamped together. Plant specimens are placed inside the sheets between the two boards. The clamps are then tightened to firmly hold the boards together.
2. Under a pile of books   A simple and easy way to press plants is to place the plants arranged between newspapers under a pile of books. Several thick telephone books or the equivalent weight in other books is appropriate.
3. Under the mattress   If you are only pressing a few plants they can be arranged in newspaper and placed between the mattress and base of the bed.
4. Inside a book   Smaller specimens can be simply

stuck on a loose sheet of paper (attach with sticky tape). The sheet can then be placed in the middle of a thick book and left for a time. Plants treated this way usually keep their original appearance, or close to it, for at least a few months. Drier foliage plants such as eucalypts press well this way.

## Herbal Fragrances

Beautiful fragrances enhance the attractiveness of both people and places. We all like a pleasant smell, particularly if it is being used to hide or overpower an unpleasant odour.

You don't have to spend lots of money or be a professional perfumer to capture and use herbal fragrances at home. You might be surprised how many things you can make from your own garden: pomanders, bath salts, scented candles, tussie mussies, potpourri, and lots more.

### Mixing Herbs

The herbs which are used in potpourri and other scented mixtures must be blended to achieve a pleasing fragrance. If you use too much of any one strongly scented herb it will overwhelm the scent of weaker herbs. The types of components should complement each other—some savoury scents do not blend well with very sweet scents.

Once you have created a pleasing scent, you may decide to add non-aromatic flower petals or attractive seed pods to enhance the colour and texture. This is particularly important for potpourris which are to be displayed in bowls.

### Pomander

A pomander makes an attractive and interesting decoration, and it's fun to make. Hung among your clothes, pomanders will impart a spicy perfume and help to repel insects. To make a pomander you will need a firm orange, lemon, or other type of citrus fruit. Make small holes through the peel with a skewer and insert whole cloves into each hole until the entire surface of the fruit is covered. Place the fruit into a container of fixative, such as powered orris root, and roll it around until it is covered. Cinnamon, nutmeg, coriander and allspice can also be mixed in the fixative. Place the fruit in a dry, well-ventilated place. After several weeks the fruit will

shrink and harden. It can then be tied with a ribbon for hanging.

### Herbal Bath Salts

Herbal bath salts are another easy way to add herbal fragrances to your bath water. They can be easily made by placing alternating layers of epsom salts and fragrant herbs in a container that can be sealed, and allowing it to sit for at least a couple of weeks. The salts can then be added to your bath water with the leaves included, or the leaves can be sieved out prior to using the salts.

### Tussie Mussie

A tussie mussie is a small posy of fragrant and colourful flowers and herbs. Traditional tussie mussies are made using a rosebud as the centrepiece surrounded by rings of dried and fresh herbs and other small fragrant flowers. The stems are secured by colourful ribbons. Once the fragrance starts to fade, sprinkle pure herb oil onto the posy to give a long-lasting fragrance.

### Scented Candles

To make scented candles melt paraffin wax and/or beeswax in a saucepan placed in a larger saucepan containing water. Do not melt the wax directly over a hot flame. As the wax melts, add aromatic herb oil or powdered herbs.

Pour the melted wax into a slightly warm mold containing a piece of candle wick. The wick should touch the bottom of the mold and protrude 1.5–2 cm above the poured wax. After the wax has completely set, remove the mold. Use scissors or glass cutters to remove plastic and tapered glass molds; remove straight-edged open molds by briefly dipping in warm water—the candle should then easily slide out. Allow the candle to stand for a short time before using.

Lavender, sage, rosemary, clove, mint and citronella are popular herbs to use in scented candles. Molds, wax and candle wicks can be purchased from craft shops, or you can make your own molds using old glass jars, empty waxed milk cartons or plastic containers.

### Potpourri

Potpourri is a mixture of dried fragrant and colourful herbs. While many people use potpourris to create pleasant fragrances in the house, others simply like them for their visual effect. A potpourri is an inexpensive but effective way to add charm and character to a room. Some potpourris have the additional benefit of acting as an insect repellant.

Potpourri is a mixture of three things:

1. Dried herbs—stems, flowers, leaves, bark and seeds.
2. Fixative—used to help 'fix' or hold the scents in the mixture.
3. Oils—these are not always necessary, but scented oils will strengthen the fragrance. Oils are often added to old potpourris to renew their scent.

### Fixatives

As a rule use 1 teaspoon of powdered fixative or several teaspoons of chopped dried fixative to 1 litre (in volume) of potpourri mixture.

Common fixatives are:

• **Orris root** This is the dried, powdered root of *Iris germanica*. Orris root powder can be purchased from craft shops.
• **Citrus peel** Dried, chopped skin of orange, lemon, grapefruit or any other citrus.
• **Sandlewood** Shavings from the bark of the sandlewood tree.
• **Gum benzoin** A tree resin, sold in craft shops.

Other fixatives are calamus root, wood chips from cedar, roots of the grass *Andropogon*, and clary sage.

### Sachets

Dried herbs can be sown into cloth sachets, bags or small pillows, and hung in cupboards, placed in the bed, on tables or anywhere else you desire to impart their scent.

Sleep pillows contain herbs which have a calming effect on the body and help induce sleep. A small sleep pillow placed under your normal bed pillow will help cure insomnia.

Sachets containing herbs which help clear the nasal passages can be placed in the bedroom to alleviate flu and cold symptoms.

## Dried Herbs to use in potpourri and sachets

| | |
|---|---|
| Basil | Spicy-scented leaves. Purple-leaved form adds colour. |
| Cardamon | Very fragrant seeds. |
| Cinnamon | Dried scented bark. |
| Clary sage | Seeds and flowers have a stronger scent than normal sage. |
| Citrus | Chopped dried leaves often used in potpourri, and in pillows to help breathing. |
| Costmary | Leaves are commonly placed between linen to impart scent. |
| Dianthus | Dried flowers provide excellent colour and a mild scent. |
| Hollyhock | Dried flowers are added to potpourri for colour only. |
| Hops | Dried hops are used in sleep pillows. |
| Lavender | Dried fragrant leaves and flowers. Half-open flowers from English lavender have the best scent. Dried lavender is placed amongst clothes to control moths. |
| Lemon verbena | Leaves have a delicate lemon scent. Do not mix with strongly-scented herbs. |
| Lemon balm | Dried leaves are excellent in potpourri or healing sachets. |
| Marjoram | Dried leaves, stems and flowers. |
| Mints | Peppermint is excellent for head colds. Other mints can be used sparingly in potpourri. |
| Muellin | Dried flowers add colour to potpourri. |
| Rose | Dried flowers, petals and flower buds from scented varieties. |
| Scented geraniums | Many different types are available, leaf scents ranging from pine and lime to peppermint and spice. Flowers can be dried, but they are not always colourful. |
| Southernwood | Dried leaves used as a moth repellent. |
| Tansy | Dried leaves used to repel insects, particularly flies |
| Thyme | Dry and strip leaves from the stems. |
| Violets | Dried flowers used for both colour and scent. |

## Insect-repelling Sachets

Any of the following herbs can be dried and mixed in whatever combination you choose: Lavender, costmary, southernwood, rue, rosemary, mint and powdered cloves.

# Extracting Herb Scents

1. Soak scented flowers or leaves in water in a warm place out of direct sunlight for a few days. Top up with fresh flowers or leaves every few days. A film of scented oil will develop on the surface of the water from where it can be collected.

2. Soak scented leaves or petals in a non-aromatic oil such as olive oil or safflower oil. Seal in a bottle and place in a warm, dark place for 2 days. Strain the plant material and repeat the procedure—oil will take on the scent of the plant and increase in strength the more times you repeat the procedure.

# Lavender Crafts

Lavender is perhaps one of the best loved fragrances and can be used in many different ways in both crafts and cosmetics.

The best lavender species for oil production are English lavender (*Lavandula angustifolia*) and *Lavandula latifolia*. English lavender has the purest lavender scent and is generally free from the camphor odour which taints all other lavenders. *Lavandula latifolia*, although tainted by camphor, still has an attractive strong rich scent. French lavender (*Lavandula dentata*) is also often used in home crafts.

## Simple ways to use lavender

• Plant a lavender bush near your laundry. After washing, drape your clothes over the bush to dry. The lavender scent will be imparted into the garments.
• Tie a bunch of lavender flowers together and hang in the bathroom to freshen the air.
• Fill a small paper bag with freshly picked lavender flowers and place in a drawer or wardrobe to repel moths and silverfish.

## Lavender Bath Elixir

*1/2 cup lavender flowers      1 teaspoon epsom salts*
*1/4 cup comfrey leaves*

Mix the lavender, comfrey and epsom salts and tie in a muslin cloth. Pour 1 litre of boiling water over the cloth slowly, catching it in a bucket. Sit the bag of herbs in the water for about 30 minutes and then use the full amount in the bath.

## Lavender Massage Oil

Add a handful of fresh lavender flowers to 1 litre of non-aromatic vegetable oil, e.g. olive oil. Leave standing in a warm position in direct sunlight for 4 days. Strain off the flowers through a muslin cloth and collect the oil. If necessary, the procedure can be repeated several times until a strong lavender scent develops in the oil.

## Lavender Sachets

Lavender sachets are used to scent cupboards and linen drawers. They can be made in a variety of ways:

## Lavender bags

1. Cut out desired cotton shapes—circles, squares and hearts are popular.
2. Sew around three edges, leaving one edge open.
3. Place dried lavender flowers in the bag.
4. Sew up open edge and sew lace around the edge of the bag.
5. Decorate with ribbon.

## Lavender wreaths.

A small cloth wreath makes a delightful Christmas decoration.
1. Cut 10 circles of coloured fabric, each 4–5 cm diameter.
2. Gather each circle around the edge, turning under the hem as you go.
3. Run a strong thread through the hem.
4. Place 3 cotton balls and 1 teaspoon of dried lavender in each circle and gently pull threads tightly to make a little ball.
5. Tie securely.
6. Using strong thread string the balls into a circle by running the needle through the two end balls.
7. Pull the thread tight and knot securely.
8. Finish with a tight bow to hang your wreath.

## Hanky sachet

A hanky sachet is a lovely gift which can be made within a few minutes. Simply fill a pretty floral hanky with lavender and tie the open ends with antique lace, silk cord or ribbon.

## Scented clothes hanger

1. Select a plain wooden hanger or a plastic hanger without bars.
2. Measure from the centre of the hanger to the end.
3. Cut fabric about 5 cm wide and 4 cm longer than this length.
4. Sew right sides together, fold and stitch to make a tube which is open at one end and closed at the other.
5. Turn fabric right side out and slip over one end of hanger.
6. Repeat for the other side.
7. Pack each tube with dried lavender and polyfibre filling, allowing enough fabric at the centre to form a seam.
8. Stitch open ends together.
9. Wrap the hook wth lace or ribbon and glue into position.
10. Decorate hanger with lace or ribbons.

## Lavender letters

Victorian ladies used to perfume their correspondence with small lavender-filled bags. Your friends will appreciate this lovely idea when they receive your scented cards and letters.
1. Cut 2 organdy squares, 4–5 cm diameter.
2. Machine-stitch the squares together on 3 sides, allowing for a 2 cm margin.
3. Open the remaining edge and pack with lavender.
4. Sew up the remaining edge.
5. Finish the edges with pinking shears.
6. Tie a ribbon in the shape of a bow and sew the the ribbon over the corner where stitching terminates.

## Rose Crafts

Roses have a particularly important place in the herb garden. As well as adding beauty to the garden, roses have many useful properties. Scented rose petals are the main ingredient of traditional potpourris; rose fruits (i.e. rose hips) are a commercial source of vitamin C and are often used to flavour herbal teas; and rose water, made from the petals, has been used as a gargle for treating sore throats or mouth sores and as an astringent skin wash.

## Using Roses in Potpourri

The scent of roses can be added to potpourri in two ways:
1. As a rose oil: This can be puchased at a craft shop, or made by soaking rose petals in safflower oil for a week, then straining off the petals before use.
2. As dried petals: Spread petals on wire racks, or on absorbent paper on a bench, preferably in a dry, dark room.

## Rose Tea Tonic

According to Joseph Meyer in his book *The Herbalist*, rose tea has a calming effect, increases the secretion of urine and has an astringent effect on the mouth and skin. He recommends using sweet briar (*Rosa canina*) to make a tonic.

To make rose tea tonic place a teaspoon of petals in a cup of boiling water and stand for an hour. Remove the petals before drinking the cold tea.

## Rose Water

Bruise fragrant rose petals and cover with water in a saucepan. Heat gently for a few minutes. Strain off the petals and save the fragrant water.

## Dried Flowers

Some flowers dry easily and retain an attractive shape and colour for a long period of time. Dried flowers can be used to make permanent floral arrangements or added to potpourri.

## Dried flowers for you to grow

| Plant | Height | Flower Colour | Stage to pick flowers |
|---|---|---|---|
| Amaranth (*Amaranthus*) | 0.3–1 m | Varies | When seed heads form |
| Bee balm (*Monarda didyma*) | 0.3 m | Brown | Seed pod fully developed |
| *Calocephalus brownii* | to 1.5 m | Silver | Flowers partly opened |
| *Calocephalus citreus* | 0.3 m | Yellow | Flowers partly opened |
| Feverfew (*Chrysanthemum parthenium*) | 0.5 m | White | Buds tight, just beginning to open |
| Gypsophila | 0.1–0.4 m | White | Flowers fully opened |
| *Helichrysum acuminatum* | to 25 cm | Gold | Buds starting to open |
| *Helichrysum apiculatum* | 10–50 cm | Yellow | Buds starting to open |
| *Helichrysum baxterii* | 20–40 cm | White | Buds starting to open |
| *Helichrysum* 'Dargen Hill' | to 1 m | Yellow | Buds starting to open |
| *Helichrysum bracteatum* | 0.3–1.5m | Varies | Buds starting to open |
| *Helichrysum diosmifolium* | 2 m | White/pink | Unopened buds |
| *Helichrysum viscosum* | to 0.5 m | Yellow | Buds starting to open |
| *Helipterum roseum* | 0.2 m | Pink | Buds starting to open |
| Lavender | to 1.4 m | Blue | Flowers fully opened |
| Lavender cotton (*Santolina*) | 0.6 m | Yellow | Flowers fully opened |
| Love-in-a-mist (*Nigella*) | 0.5 m | Pink/green | Seed pod fully developed |
| *Lunaria annua* | 75 cm | Brown | Seed pod fully developed |
| Quaking grass (*Briza*) | 20–60 cm | White | Early stages of flower development |
| Rue (*Ruta graveolens*) | 60 cm | Brown | Seed pod fully developed |
| Scabiosa | 45–90 cm | Varies | After petals drop |
| Statice (*Limonium*) | 45 cm | Varies | Flowers fully opened |
| Tansy (*Tanacetum vulgare*) | 60 cm | Yellow | Flowers fully opened |
| Wormwood (*Artemisia*) | 60–90 cm | Grey | Flowers fully opened |
| Yarrow (*Achillea*) | 8–60 cm | Varies | Flowers fully opened |

For most flowers, all you need do is pick them at the correct stage of growth and hang them upside down to dry in a reasonably dark, dry and well-ventilated room.

## Preserving dried flowers

There are two important factors to remember when you dry flowers:
1. Flowers must be free of moisture at the time of harvesting.
2. Only use flowers which are completely free of blemishes.

## Air Drying

This is the easiest method of drying flowers. Strip the leaves from the stems, place into small bunches and tie the ends of each bunch with string. Hang the bunches in a dark, well-ventilated room or cupboard for several weeks. Alternatively, place the stems loosely on racks which allow good air circulation.

Check the drying flowers regularly—over-dry flowers can become too brittle. When the stems can be snapped, they are dry enough. Store in hanging bunches or in boxes.

## Desiccants

Desiccants are substances which absorb moisture from the plant. They are most commonly used to dry large individual blooms or fragile flower heads. Silica gel is the fastest method and gives good colour preservation. It is an expensive desiccant, although the crystals can be reused (dry the crystals in oven at 120° C for 30 minutes). Sand is cheap and easy to use. Use fine, clean river sand—fragile flowers may be crushed by heavy sand. Borax can also be used.

Method
1. Cover the bottom of an airtight container with the desiccant to a depth of 3 cm.
2. Place flower heads on top of the covering layer. Flowers should not be touching each other.

3. Gently pour desiccant over the petals. The entire surface of the flower should be in contact with the desiccant—a toothpick or small paintbrush can be used to hold the petals apart.

4. Seal the container and store in a warm, dry place.

5. When the petals feel dry and crisp, remove the flowers and brush off the desiccant. Drying should take around 2–3 days for small flowers; larger flowers will take at least a week.

## Glycerine

Flowers which tend to become too brittle when air dried can be preserved in glycerine—this keeps them moist and avoids brittleness. Add 1 part glycerine to 2 parts warm water, mix vigorously and stand freshly cut stems in this solution in a cool, dim place. Leave for 2 weeks; top up solution if necessary.

## Wiring and Taping

Before drying, flowers can be wired to prevent drooping and to enable the flower heads to last longer. Wiring is also used to create visual effects in dried arrangements, e.g. curved stems. Cut the stem to about 1/2 cm length. Using florist's wire, or a similar flexible wire, push the wire up through the stem until it reaches the flower head and is firmly lodged there. When the flower head has shrunk onto the wire (around 2-3 weeks), cover the bare wire with self-adhesive florist's tape.

# 6 Directory of Herbs

Note: The botanical naming of many common herb plants is often quite confusing. The names listed below follow those in the botanical reference *Hortus Third*, prepared by the staff of th: L.H. Bailey Hortorium at Cornell University and published by Macmillan. The exception to this is where alternative family names are commonly used—in these cases both family names are listed.

**Allium**   *Allium* species   Liliaceae

*At a glance*
Number of species: Approximately 400.
Origin: Widespread, mainly Northern Hemisphere.
Hardiness: Generally very hardy.
Habit: Clump-forming perennials.
Growth rate: Fast

*Culture*
Excellent drainage, dry to moist, but not wet soil.
Most varieties prefer full sun—heavy shade reduces the crop.
Good air movement around foliage is important.
pH 6.0–7.0.
Organic soils give the best results.
Responds to feeding, but generally avoid high nitrogen fertilisers. Balanced, slow release fertilisers are best. Most varieties are propagated by seed or division.

*Herb species*
Chives   *Allium Schoenoprasum*
A bulb-forming perennial with thin, hollow, grass-like leaves which die back in winter. Chives require filtered sun and fertile, moist soil. Propagate by seed or division.
The leaves are used to flavour savoury foods, e.g. meats and vegetables, or chopped as a garnish. Also used as a companion plant.

Garlic chives   *Allium tuberosum*
Garlic chives are evergreen and differ to common chives in appearance and fragrance. The leaves are used in the same way as common chives but in smaller quantities as they have a stronger flavour and a slight garlic taste. Heat tends to destroy the flavour—they are best mixed into hot dishes after cooking, just prior to serving.

Elephant garlic   *Allium giganteum*
A clump-forming plant, to 1 m tall. The leaves have a milder flavour than common garlic. Both the leaves and bulbs can be harvested and used fresh or dried in cooking.

Garlic   *Allium sativum*
A hardy clump-forming plant to 0.7 m tall which dies back in cold weather, then regrows in the warmer months.
Garlic prefers rich, moist, fertile, sandy soil. It is important to keep the soil weed-free. Propagate by dividing the root system or cloves in early autumn or early spring. Best planted in autumn about a month before the first frosts. Plant 4–5 cm diameter cloves approximately 10–12 cm apart in the rows; the spacing between rows should be 30–40 cm.

Leaves and roots, being high in sulphur, are a natural antibiotic and can be used as a medicine for people and animals, or as a spray to control fungal diseases on plants.

### Commercial Production

Weed control is particularly important. In most large commercial crops this is achieved by careful timing of herbicide applications. Weeds are also controlled by shallow cultivation.

Approximately 400 kg (900 pounds) of cloves are needed to plant 0.45 ha (one acre). Seed-planting machines are used to plant large scale crops.

Garlic respond to fertilisers, but do not require as heavy feeding as other crops. Growers in some areas use soil and tissue culture testing to help determine the type and timing of fertilisers.

Clove development commences when the leaves stop growing. To obtain maximum yields, maximum top growth needs to be developed and the upper 60 cm of soil should remain moist but not wet.

### Seed Storage

Cloves should be stored at 0-2° C. Storing at too high or low a temperature can cause side shooting and delayed maturity. A pre-cooling treatment at 19° C for two weeks will result in the plants maturing two to four weeks earlier once cloves are removed from storage and planted out.

### Harvesting

Care must be taken to cure and dry garlic before storage. If harvested into bins where humidity becomes too high, rot can set in. Bruising can occur if harvested by machines operating at too high a speed (or with badly designed harvesting machines). Varieties vary in their keeping quality.

### Onion  *Allium cepa*

The common onion is a versatile and often overlooked addition to the herb garden. Used medicinally, onions combat fungal and bacterial diseases, help reduce cholesterol levels, and according to some sources, lower blood pressure. Its culinary uses in flavouring savoury dishes are well known. The flower heads can be used in dried arrangements and the bulb skins are excellent for dyeing wool.

Shallots *Allium ascalonicum* (considered by some authorities to be a cultigen of *Allium cepa*)
A bulbous plant growing in clumps to 0.6 m tall. Prefers full sun and well-drained, fertile, sandy soil. Propagate by dividing clumps and planting bulblets

Onion (*Allium cepa*)

in early spring.
Used in butters, seasonings and to flavour savoury dishes.

### Aloe  *Aloe* species  Liliaceae

*At a glance*
Number of species: Over 200.
Origin: Mainly dry parts of Africa.
Hardiness: Very hardy in warm frost-free areas. Many varieties are frost tender.
Habit: Usually clump forming, without stems, ranging from small succulents to tall tree-like plants.
Growth rate: Medium to very fast.

*Aloe vera*

### Culture

Avoid excess water around roots (waterlogged soils can cause root rot).

Few pests and diseases.
Propagate by division and replanting suckers.

*Herb species*
Aloe vera   *Aloe barbadensis*
A succulent lily with rosette leaves to 1 m. Very drought tolerant, suited to dry, gravelly soils in full sun. Propagate by dividing small offshoots from main stems.
Juices from leaves are used as a tonic and as a healing ointment for burns and wounds. To make a tincture, cover chopped leaves with methylated spirits and store in an airtight container.

**Angelica**   *Angelica* species   Apiaceae or Umbelliferae

*At a glance*
Number of species: Approximately 50.
Origin: Mainly temperate areas in the Northern Hemisphere.
Hardiness: Hardy
Habit: Perennial herbs.
Growth rate: Very fast.

*Culture*
Moist but well-drained soil. Some species prefer wet soil.
Full or filtered sun.
Protection from strong winds.
Feed regularly.
Propagate by seed in late summer (occasionally by division).

*Herb species*
Angelica   *Angelica archangelica*
A hardy, fast growing herb to 2 m tall. Grows fast over spring, dies down to the roots in winter. Lives 2-3 years only.
Roots, leaf stalks and stems are split and candied. Stems and roots are eaten raw in Scandinavia. Leaflets are sometimes boiled and eaten like spinach (but they are bitter). Fruits are used in herbal medicines.

Shiny leaf angelica   *Angelica pachycarpa*
Grows to 1 m tall and has particularly attractive foliage which is used as a garnish. This species is generally hardier than the more commonly grown *Angelica archangelica.*

Amercian angelica   *Angelica atropurpurea*
A more open bush to 1.2 m tall with dark purple leaves and a strong smelling, poisonous root. Prefers moist soil. Foliage has been used for medicinal

purposes.

Wild angelica   *Angelica sylvestris*
Grows to 1.3 m tall with white to pink flowers. The flowers have been used to give a yellow dye.

**Anise**   *Pimpinella* species   Apiaceae or Umbelliferae

*At a glance*
Number of species: 140; common anise is the only species commonly grown as a herb.
Origin: Eurasia and Africa.
Hardiness: Fairly hardy.
Habit: Small plants to 1 m.
Growth rate: Fast under good conditions.

*Culture*
Grown outdoors in warm areas or in greenhouses.
Requires well-drained, fertile soil.
Sunny but protected position.
Propagate by seed in mid-spring. Can be sown directly into garden in final position.

*Herb species*
Common anise   *Pimpinella anisum*
An annual, slightly tender, to 0.6 m tall. The seeds are used for flavouring cakes, bread, sweets and liqueurs.

Water pimpernel   *Pimpinella saxifraga*
Closely related to anise, to 90 cm tall, with white flower heads and leaves similar to salad burnet. Small doses of the foliage or root are used to make a medicinal tea which stimulates secretions of body fluids.

**Giant or Anise Hyssop**   *Agastache or Brittonastrum* species   Lamiaceae or Labiatae

*At a glance*
Number of species: Approximately 30.
Origin: North America, Mexico and Asia.
Hardiness: Hardy.
Habit: Tall perennial herbs
Growth rate: Fast.

*Culture*
Full sun to filtered light position.
Average soil.
Use as a border plant.
Propagate by division.

*Herb species*
Anise hyssop   *Agastache Foeniculum*
A perennial from North America, growing to 0.9 m

tall. Spikes of small lavender flowers appear during summer.

Foliage has a strong, sweet scent and is used in cold drinks and fruit salads or as a hot tea. Good bee attractant.

**Mosquito plant**   *Agastache cana*

Woody plant to 70 cm bearing pink flowers from southwest USA.

**Artemisia**   *Artemisia*   species   Asteraceae   or Compositae

*At a glance*

Number of species: Approximately 200.
Natural habitat: Mainly dry climates.
Hardiness: Hardy to very hardy.
Habit: Perennial herbs and shrubs.
Growth rate: Fast.

*Culture*

Prefers dry to just moist soil with excellent drainage.
Prefers full sun.
Most species are adapted to extremes of temperature, but some do not tolerate high humidity.
Most species have few pests or diseases.
Need regular pruning to maintain shape.
Normally propagate by cuttings; sometimes by seed or division.

*Herb species*

**Sweet wormwood**   *Artemisia annua*

An annual growing to 3 m tall. The leaves are sweetly aromatic, up to 8 cm long. Flowers are white to yellow.

**Southernwood**   *Artemisia Abrotanum*

A very hardy woody shrub, with aromatic fine blue-green leaves. Grows to 1.5 m tall in temperate climates. Dried foliage is used in potpourri and as a moth repellant. Also used medicinally and for culinary purposes, e.g. fresh leaves are used to flavour roast lamb. Said by some to be a companion plant for control of aphis.

**Wormwood**   *Artemisia Absinthium*

A woody shrub to 2 m tall and several metres diameter. Foliage is silver-grey. Very hardy, adapting to both cold and hot conditions. Drought tolerant once established.
Dried leaves can be used in potpourri. Leaves are also used in making vermouth.
Wormwood has been used medicinally, however oil from the leaves is toxic and there are documented cases of serious poisoning. The leaves are said to repel slugs, snails, snakes, moths and butterflies. A tea made from wormwood can be sprayed to control aphis.

**Tarragon**   *Artemisia Dracunculus*

A semi-hardy rhizomatous perennial which dies back to the roots over winter. Grows to 1.5 m tall in the warmer months. The leaves are linear to lanceolate, up to 10 cm long.
Depending on variety, tarragon can be almost scentless to strongly aromatic.
Tarragon leaves are commonly used as a seasoning or in herb vinegars.

**White mugwort**   *Artemisia lactiflora*

An erect, herbaceous shrub to 1.7 m tall. The lower leaves are up to 20 cm long and are either toothed or lobed in shape. White flowers.

**Wormseed**   *Artemisia maritima*

A strongly aromatic small shrub to 70 cm tall. Leaves to 5 cm long, hairy on top and bottom. Flowers yellowish to reddish.

**Roman wormwood**   *Artemisia pontica*

An erect shrub to 1.2 m tall. Leaves to 4 cm long, hairy and grey on both sides. Flowers whitish-yellow.

**Mugwort**   *Artemisia vulgaris*

An aromatic shrub to 2 m tall. Leaves are divided but mainly oval in outline.
Dried leaves have been used as a condiment, and mugwort tea has been used medicinally, although recent evidence has indicated problems with taking mugwort internally. Mugwort baths and dried mugwort in a sleep pillow are said to be very relaxing. In England leaves are used in making ale.

**Balm**   *Melissa* species   Lamiaceae or Labiatae

*At a glance*

Number of species: 3.
Origin: Europe to central Asia.
Hardiness: Very hardy except for extremes of hot and cold.
Habit: Perennial clumps.
Growth rate: Fast.

*Culture*

Grows in most soils; prefers moist soil.
Prefers a well lit position but withstands some shade.
Cut flowering stems as soon as flowers finish to prevent self seeding.
Harvest for drying when in full flower.

Propagate by seed, division or cuttings.

### Herb species

Lemon balm    *Melissa officinalis*

Clumps can grow to 0.7 m or more tall, but will die down over winter. Large quantities of seed are produced. In temperate climates the seeds germinate readily, sometimes making it a weed. Withstands heavy pruning. Fresh foliage is used as a lemon substitute to flavour drinks, sweets or anywhere else that lemons are used. Dried foliage is used in potpourri.

Variegated lemon balm    *Melissa officinalis variegata*

A gold and green-leaved form of lemon balm. Very hardy herb to 0.5 m tall, dying back to the roots in cold weather and regrowing in spring. The gold foliage is bright in sunny conditions but can revert to green in shaded conditions or in the cooler months. Leaves can be used in cooking as a lemon substitute.

## Basil    *Ocimum* species    Lamiaceae or Labiatae

### At a glance

Number of species: Approximately 150.
Origin: Europe.
Hardiness: Tender foliage, particularly when young.
Habit: Small shrubs, mostly annuals.
Growth rate: Fast.

### Culture

Needs fertile, constantly moist but well-drained soil.
Requires a protected warm sunny site.
Can be devastated by chewing insects or snails.
Propagates easily from seed in mid-spring; protection from late frosts may be required.

### Herb species

Common or Sweet basil    *Ocimum basilicum*

The most commonly grown basil; a tender annual, to 0.3 m tall. A large variety is available from 0.1 to 0.8 m tall; foliage colour and flavours also vary. To harvest, cut stems close to ground at flowering time. Regrowth will provide one or two additional crops in a season.

The pungently flavoured leaves enhance the flavour of savoury cooking, particularly French and Italian tomato dishes and Indian curries. Basil is also one of several ingredients in Chartreuse liqueur. Foliage can be dried and used in potpourri and added to hair rinses, herbal baths and a range of cosmetics, e.g. soaps, perfumes, shampoos.

Lemon-scented basil    *Ocimum basilicum* 'Citriodorum'

A variety of the sweet basil with a lemon scent to the leaves. Growth habit and plant features are similar to sweet basil. Leaves are used to flavour drinks and added to potpourri.

### *Ocimum gratissimum*

A less commonly grown basil, to 1.8 m tall, suited to warmer climates. The pale yellow flower heads and scented foliage are used in potpourri.

Hoary basil    *Ocimum canum*

Grows to 70 cm tall. Features white flowers and scented foliage.

## Bay tree    *Laurus nobilis*    Lauraceae

### At a glance

Origin: Mediterranean region.
Hardiness: Hardy.
Habit: Medium to large aromatic tree, often with suckers at the base.
Growth rate: Slow.

### Culture

Requires full sun.
Prefers cooler climates. Frost resistant.
Deep soil with good drainage and medium fertility.
Frequently attacked by scale insects.
Propagate by cuttings or seed.
Makes a good tub plant.

*Laurus nobilis* is an hardy evergreen tree to 30 m tall with a 6–9 m spread, although in cultivation plants are generally much smaller. Leaves are elliptical, thick, glossy and aromatic, up to 10 cm long.

In the average home garden bay is best grown in a container to keep it small. They can be easily pruned to maintain a compact shape. Plants may be slightly tender when young but mature trees will tolerate frosts. In early Roman times, the leaves were formed into wreaths to crown heroes. Nowadays the leaves are usually dried and used as a bouquet garni to flavour savoury meats and soups. Oil, extracted from the purple-black berries produced by female trees, has also been used in perfumes.

There are a number of cultivars including 'Angustifolia', the willow leaf bay, which has narrow lanceolate leaves; 'Aurea' which has yellowish-golden coloured leaves; and 'Undulata' which has leaves with wavy margins.

**Bergamot**  *Monarda didyma*  Lamiaceae or Labiatae

*At a glance*
Origin: North America through to Mexico.
Hardiness: Very hardy and adaptable.
Habit: Small perennial.
Growth rate: Rapid.

*Culture*
Prefers partial shade and a protected position.
Requires moist and very fertile soil to crop well.
Propagate by division, or sometimes seed; when dividing plants retain outer sections of clumps and discard the centres.

A hardy herbaceous perennial, to 0.9 m tall, with attractive red flowers.
Bergamot is grown commercially for the essential oils and edible leaves. The cut leaf market has potential, but the major market is for the oil which is used in creams, perfumes, lotions and soaps.
The leaves are aromatic and when infused with boiling water induce deep relaxing sleep. Leaves are also used in potpourri and shredded in salads.
There are a number of cultivars with flowers in shades of red, pink and violet.

**Borage**  *Borago officinalis*  Boraginaceae

*At a glance*
Origin: Mediterranean region.
Hardiness: Fairly hardy.
Habit: Small clumping annual plant.
Growth rate: Vigorous in warmer months.

*Culture*
Prefers fertile, alkaline soil with good drainage.
Waterlogged soils will result in rot and death of plant.
Grows in full sun to partly shaded position.
May need to control grasshoppers and other chewing insects.
Propagate by seed sown 0.3 m apart, or by division or cuttings.
Good container plant.

Borage is a hardy annual, to 0.6 m tall. In the past borage has been widely used medicinally, but some herbalists warn that long-term use may affect the liver. Fresh leaves are used raw in salads or cooked with vegetables. Dried and frozen leaves do not keep well, but can be preserved in vinegar. The edible flowers may be candied and used as a garnish or dried and added to potpourri. A good bee attractant.

**Boronia**  *Boronia* species  Rutaceae

*At a glance*
Number of species: 60–70.
Natural habitat: Australia wide, usually in coastal regions.
Hardiness: Variable.
Habit: Woody shrubs to 1.5 m tall. A few annuals exist.
Growth rate: Fast in warm months but slow in winter when they almost stop growing.

*Culture*
Perfect drainage is essential.
Cool, moist root run required. In exposed soils grow beside a log or rock, and cover with mulch.
Most species prefer full sun.
Annual or twice yearly pruning will extend the life-span of plants. Prune hard in the first year.
Scale can be a major problem.
Boronias often give best results in infertile, slightly acid soils.
Propagate by semi-hardwood cuttings

*Herb species*
Brown boronia  *Boronia megastigma*
Strongly scented flowers appear during late winter and spring. Foliage is also scented. Flowers can be dried and used in pot pourri, or put through a distillation process to extract the valuable oil for use in cosmetics, e.g. perfumes, soaps, bath salts.

Red boronia  *Boronia heterophylla*
Suited to moist, acid soils. Good drainage is essential, but the soil should not be allowed to dry out. A cool and protected position is preferred (plants will tolerate full sun in cool coastal climates, but may require semi-shade in hotter areas).

**Burnet, salad**  *Poterium Sanguisorba* or *Sanguisorba minor* (classification is unclear)  Rosaceae

*At a glance*
Origin: Europe, West Asia and northern Africa.
Hardiness: Hardy; drought tolerant.
Habit: Low growing perennial.
Growth Rate: Fast.

*Culture*
Requires light, well-drained soil.
Do not allow soil to dry out to wilting stage.
Propagate by seed or root division.

A low growing hardy plant to 0.9 m tall. The leaves

have a cucumber flavour and are used in salads, salad dressings, herbal butters and vinegars. Drying destroys the flavour.

## Calendula or Pot Marigold *Calendula officinalis* Asteraceae or Compositae

*At a glance*
Origin: Southern and central Europe.
Hardiness: Hardy and adaptable small plants.
Habit: Small annual.
Growth rate: Fast growing.

*Culture*
Sunny site.
Well-drained soil.
Need to be replanted each season.
Propagate by seeds.

Annual herb to 40 cm tall. Golden or yellow daisy flowers are borne throughout summer and autumn. Best floral displays are obtained in cool temperate areas. Frost resistant.
Edible fresh petals can be used as a colourful garnish in salads, candied for cake decoration, or boiled to make a yellow dye. Petals dried and put through a blender makes a powder which can be substituted for saffron in cooking. Petals frequently used in pot-pourri. Often used as a companion plant to deter nematodes.

## Cardamon *Elettaria Cardamomum* Zingiberaceae

*At a glance*
Origin: India.
Hardiness: Hardy if provided with frost protection.
Habit: Herbaceous plant with underground rhizome.
Growth rate: Vigorous in summer. Slow growth or dormancy in winter (depending on climate).

*Culture*
Prefers moist fertile soils.
Shady site with protection from hot midday sun.
Grows best in warm climates, otherwise glasshouse conditions are required.
Prone to leaf attack by chewing insects.
Waterlogged conditions may result in rhizome rot and death.
Propagate by division of rhizomes or by seed.

Leafy perennial to 2 m tall. Highly scented seeds are used in herbal medicines, chewed as a breath freshener, and added to flavour alcoholic drinks, sweets, cakes, biscuits and fruit salads.

## Caraway *Carum Carvi* Apiaceae or Umbelliferae

*At a glance*
Origin: Europe.
Hardiness: Extremely hardy.
Habit: Rosette-forming herb with tall flowers.
Growth rate: Fast during growing season.

*Culture*
Loose, moist but well-drained soil.
Requires high light.
If planted too late, the plant may go to seed early, but produce a poor crop.
Propagate by seed in early autumn and spring in mild areas.

Attractive hardy herb to 0.6 metres tall. The small narrow black seeds give a distinctive flavour to cakes and breads.

## Catnip *Nepeta Cataria* Lamiaceae or Labiatae

*At a glance*
Origin: Eurasia.
Hardiness: Hardy.
Habit: Low growing herb, often used as a ground cover.
Growth rate: Fast during the growing season.

*Culture*
Requires rich sandy, moist soil.
Grow in partial shade with protection from hot sun and strong winds.
Propagate by root division, seeds, layering or stem cuttings in spring or autumn.

An attractive aromatic grey-green, slightly hairy-leaved herb, to 0.6 m tall. Spike-like flower head with small white and purple flowers in summer.
Leaves and shoots are used to flavour savoury dishes or to make a tea. Often grown to attract cats. The cultivar 'Citriodora' has lemon-scented foliage.

## Chamomile *Anthemis* and *Matricaria* species Asteraceae or Compositae

*At a glance*
Number of species: There are three genus types in the chamomile group.
Hardiness: All species are fairly hardy.
Habit: Mat-forming to small upright plants. Annuals or perennials.
Growth rate: Rapid during growing season.

*Coleus caninus*

Comfrey (*Symphytum officinale*)

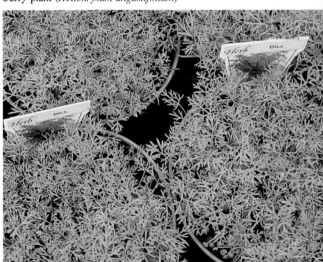

Curry plant (*Helichrysum angustifolium*)

Dianthus
Evening primrose (*Oenothera biennis*)

Dill (*Anethium graveolens*)
Bronze fennel (*Foeniculum vulgare* 'Purpureum')

Fenugreek sprouts

Feverfew (*Chrysanthemum parthenium*)

Garlic cloves

Garlic growing as a companion plant to peach tree.
Ginger (*Zingiber officinale*)

Germander (*Teucrium chamaedrys*)
Herb robert

## Culture

All species require good drainage.

Prefers full sun. Partial shade can be tolerated in warm hot areas.

Requires moist soil with large amounts of organic matter added.

Tolerates hot conditions.

Propagate by seed, division or cuttings.

### Herb species

Lawn or Roman chamomile  *Anthemis nobile*

An evergreen mat-forming perennial with fine bright green leaves. Grows to 0.3 m tall, although it is often cut shorter and grown as a lawn. Native to western Europe, Azores and northern Africa.

Chamomile oil is used in many products including liqueurs, bath oils, cosmetics, hair dyes, mouth washes, shampoos, sunscreens, detergents, perfumes and soaps. On a worldwide basis chamomile oil is in higher demand than peppermint oil. Roman chamomile is grown commercially in Germany, Hungary, Egypt, Bulgaria, Yugoslavia, Turkey, Russia, USA and Albania. Flowers are used to make tea.

German chamomile  *Matricaria recutita*

An upright annual shrub to 0.75 m tall. Single white daisy flowers with yellow centres appear in summer. Native to Europe and western Asia.

The dried flowers are used to make the 'normal' chamomile tea which is renowned for its nerve-soothing properties. The flowers are also used in hair rinses for lightening blonde hair.

## Chervil  *Anthriscus Cerefolium*  Apiaceae or Umbelliferae

### At a glance

Origin: Europe and western Asia.

Hardiness: Hardy.

Habit: Annual plant; similar habit to parsley.

Growth rate: Rapid in spring and autumn. Occasionally dies down in summer.

### Culture

Filtered sun.

Fertile and moist but well-drained soil.

Propagate by seed sown in spring or late summer.

Annual to 0.45 m tall. Plants can grow to 60 cm, but are normally harvested at a much lower height. Chervil does not like extremes of heat or cold and is best grown as a quick crop in spring or autumn. Seed is sown direct into rows; the leaves are ready to harvest in 6–8 weeks.

It is a popular herb in Europe; demand is also increasing in Australia. Curled-leaved varieties are the most popular for use as garnishes. Fresh leaves can be harvested and used like parsley. Seeds are also used for culinary purposes, e.g. flavouring vinegar.

## Chicory  *Cichorium Intybus*  Asteraceae or Compositae

### At a glance

Origin: Northern Africa, Europe and western Asia.

Hardiness: Hardy.

Habit: Stout perennial clump-forming plant; similar to lettuce.

Growth rate: Fast.

### Culture

Soil needs to be well-drained and fertile. Do not allow soil to dry out.

Propagate by seed.

Blue flowers occur on stems up to 0.8 m tall. Leaves can be eaten fresh or cooked as a vegetable, but are bitter unless blanched. The root is used as a coffee substitute. A tea made from 1 teaspoon of dried root in 1 cup of boiling water is used medicinally to treat stomach complaints (drink cold, one mouthful up to 3 times daily).

## Chives—see Allium

## Cinnamon  *Cinnamomum zeylanicum*  Lauraceae

### At a glance

Origin: Ceylon and southwest India.

Hardiness: Temperature sensitive, needs sub-tropical to tropical conditions.

Habit: Small tree.

Growth rate: Fast in the tropics.

### Culture

Tropical or sub-tropical climate is essential.

Requires highly fertile soil with organic matter added.

Full sun when mature.

Protect from frosts.

Propagate by cuttings.

### General

Tree to 9 m tall with yellow and white flowers. Scented bark is dried to use as commercial cinnamon. Bark is also used for medicinal, culinary and aromatic purposes. It is increasingly being used in potpourri mixtures and air fresheners. Cinnamon, cloves and

Cinnamon (*Cinnamon zeylanicum*)

ginger can be simmered in a saucepan of water to freshen the air in the kitchen.

## Citrus  *Citrus* species  Rutaceae

*At a glance*

Number of species: 16.
Origin: Asia region.
Hardiness: Hardy and adaptable.
Habit: Evergreen spiny shrubs to small and medium-sized trees.
Growth rate: Usually rapid but this can depend on species or cultivar.

*Culture*

Needs fertile well-drained soils.
Full sun.
Protection from frost, insects and diseases needed for fruit and the tree.
Prevent weed growth around trunk.

*Herb varieties*

The fruit of the citrus species are well known for their juices. They are a valuable source of citric acid. The fruit peels contain essential oils and aromatic compounds and the peels of oranges and lemons are candied for use as sweets. Citrus flowers are generally fragrant and can be a valuable addition to potpourri. The leaves of some types of citrus—including lemon, lime, kumquat, grapefruit and orange—are also used to flavour soups, rice dishes and stews.
Commonly grown citrus include:
*Citrus Limon* 'Eureka'. The Eureka lemon prefers cooler climates, is thornless and bears fruit mainly in summer.
*Citrus Limon* 'Lisbon'. The Lisbon lemon prefers warmer climates than the Eureka but is adaptable. It bears mainly in winter.
*Citrus Limon* 'Meyer'. The Meyer lemon withstands cold climates and bears mainly in the late winter to early spring.
*Citrus sinensis*. Sweet oranges grow 4–8 m tall and generally prefer warmer climates. Commonly grown varieties include Navel and Valencia.
*Citrus aurantiifolia*. The sweet lime is a small to medium tree from 3 to 10 m tall, suitable for warmer climates. It is the source of lime juice.
*Fortunella japonica*. The kumquat is a medium-sized shrub to 3 m tall, with miniature orange-like fruits. It requires a warm situation and is a useful tub specimen. The fruit is used in preserves.

## Coleus  *Coleus* species  Lamiaceae or Labiatae

*At a glance*

Number of species: 150.
Origin: Americas, Angola, central Africa, India.
Hardiness: Frost tender but adaptable.
Habit: Small, low-growing annuals or perennials, usually with succulent leaves and stems.
Growth rate: Vigorous in tropical climates; medium growth in temperate areas.

*Culture*

Provide protection from frosts.
Bright light is desirable.
Fertile, moist but well-drained soil.
Propagate by cuttings.

*Herb species*

Five seasons herb  *Coleus amboinicus*
A blue-green foliage plant, spreading to 1 m or more in diameter and 10–30 cm tall. It is sensitive to extremes of cold and moisture. Foliage has a flavour similar to marjoram and can be used in meat, vegetable, soup or egg dishes. A variegated form is also available.

Dog bane  *Coleus caninus*
A blue-grey plant, 20–40 cm tall, spreading and vigorous. Grows best in warm climates. Tolerates cool temperatures but not frost. Scent from foliage repels many (but not all) dogs and cats.
This species has also been listed as *Coleus canis* and *Coleus canosus*.

## Comfrey  *Symphytum officinale*  Boraginaceae

*At a glance*

Origin: Europe and Asia
Hardiness: Hardy in warm climates. Grows well in cooler areas.

Habit: Clumping perennial up to 1 m tall (including flowers).

Growth rate: Rapid in warm climates, but slows down in winter or dies down to the roots in cold areas.

*Culture*

Prefers partial shade.

Semi-fertile, well-drained but moist soils.

Propagate by root cuttings, division or seed.

Comfrey has traditionally been used as a poultice on wounds or bruises to promote healing, though in recent years this practice has been criticised. Some experts believe it is poisonous, while others believe if taken in moderation it has many beneficial effects on the body. It is best to use this herb for external uses only such as poultices.

Comfrey is also said to speed decomposition if added to a compost heap, and has been used as a brown dye for wool (using iron as a mordant).

**Coriander** *Coriandrum sativum* Apiaceae or Umbelliferae

*At a glance*

Origin: Southern Europe.

Hardiness: Hardy.

Habit: Small annual to 90 cm tall (usually much less).

Growth rate: Fast during the growing season.

*Culture*

Requires a light, moist but well-drained soil.

Good light is essential.

Propagate by seed in spring.

Seeds are used to flavour cakes and breads. Slightly bitter leaves are used in Chinese dishes and other cooking.

**Curry Plant** *Helichrysum angustifolium* Asteraceae or Compositae

*At a glance*

Origin: Mediterranean region.

Hardiness: Hardy.

Habit: Woody perennial shrub.

Growth rate: Fast.

*Culture*

Prefers a dry, well-drained soil.

Full sun.

Propagate by seed.

Hardy perennial shrub to 75 cm tall with silver-coloured, curry-scented leaves and small gold daisy flowers. Leaves are used to flavour soups and casseroles.

**Dandelion** *Taraxacum officinale* Asteraceae or Compositae

*At a glance*

Origin: Europe and Asia; now naturalised in many countries.

Hardiness: Very hardy; usually regarded as an invasive weed.

Habit: Rosette base from which arises a tall flower stalk.

Growth rate: Rapid.

*Culture*

Very adaptable to soil types but prefers moist soils.

Adapted to grow in many climatic regions.

Part shade to full sun.

Propagate by seed (self seeds readily).

A common weed with yellow daisy flowers. The leaves are harvested like spinach. Young leaves can be chopped and added to salads—blanching makes them sweeter. Roots are dried, roasted and used as a coffee substitute.

Dandelion (*Taraxacum officinale*)

Dandelions also have a range of medicinal uses and are grown commercially in the USA and parts of Europe. The cultivated dandelion grown in these countries has been bred and developed from the wild dandelion. Seed is directly sown in rows (though seedlings will transplant), 25–30 cm apart and 45 cm between the rows. Light sandy soils are preferred. Weeds are controlled by hand cultivation.

**Dianthus** *Dianthus* species   Caryophyllaceae

*At a glance*
Number of species: 300.
Origin: Eurasia through to South Africa.
Hardiness: Hardy; prefers cool areas.
Habit: Low growing and spreading annuals or perennials.
Growth rate: Depends on species.

*Culture*
Most species prefer cool climates. Tropics are generally unsuitable.
Bright light to full sun.
Well-drained, fertile, slightly alkaline soil. If you add manure or mulch, add lime at the same time to raise the pH level.
Control of insects and fungi essential.
Propagate by seed, division, cuttings or layering.

There are many different species and varieties with bluish foliage and carnation-like scented flowers.
Dried flower heads are used in potpourri.

**Dill** *Anethum graveolens* Apiaceae or Umbelliferae

*At a glance*
Origin: Southwest Asia.
Hardiness: Hardy.
Habit: Small annual herb with delicate fern-like foliage.
Growth rate: Rapid during the growing season.

*Culture*
Part shade to full sun.
Rich soil with perfect drainage.
Late planting or dry soil will cause the flowers to bolt (i.e. turn into seed heads).
Propagate by seed sown direct in spring. Seedlings are difficult to transplant.

An annual herb to 0.9 m tall with fine, lacy foliage. Unripe seeds are used to flavour vinegar, sauerkraut and pickled cucumbers.

**Eucalypt** *Eucalyptus* species   Myrtaceae

*At a glance*
Number of species: Over 500.
Origin: Nearly all species are endemic to Australia.
Hardiness: Very hardy and adaptable.
Habit: Small to large trees.
Growth rate: Rapid once established.

*Culture*
Most species prefer full sun.
Will tolerate frost, salt wind, drought and floods providing correct species is chosen.
Adaptable to different soil types.
May need pruning as limbs fall off in strong winds.

*Herb species*
Eucalypt leaves contain oils which are used for medicinal or antiseptic purposes. The blue gum *Eucalyptus globulus* is particularly good because of its high oil content. A dwarf form of blue gum *Eucalyptus globulus compacta* is favoured in home gardens, only growing to around 6 m tall (the normal form can grow over 30 m). Regular harvesting will stimulate regrowth of lush immature blue-coloured leaves (mature leaves are green and less attractive). Foliage dries readily if hung in a dark, dry room. Leaves are often chopped to use in potpourri.

Other useful eucalypts include:
Lemon-scented gum *Eucalyptus citriodora*—the leaf scent is a mixture of eucalypt and lemon.
Blue gum *Eucalyptus globulus*—attractive blue juvenile leaves with strong, typical eucalyptus scent.
Peppermint gum *Eucalyptus nicholli*—leaves have a peppermint-gum scent.

**Evening Primrose** *Oenothera biennis* Onagraceae

*At a glance*
Origin: Eastern North America; now a naturalised weed in many countries.
Hardiness: Hardy.
Habit: Biennial weed.
Growth rate: Fast during the growing season.

*Culture*
Light shade preferred.
Moist but well-drained soil; can tolerate fairly dry conditions.
Deep friable soil is best so that the roots can be harvested.
Propagate by seed (plants will readily self-seed).

Yellow-flowering herb to 1.5 m tall. A leafy rosette is produced in the first season, followed by large cup-shaped flowers the following summer. The thick taproot can be eaten as a vegetable substitute.

**Fennel** *Foeniculum vulgare* Apiaceae or Umbelliferae

*At a glance*
Origin: Southern Europe.
Hardiness: Hardy in temperate areas.
Habit: Perennial that dies back to roots in winter in cool areas.
Growth rate: Rapid.

*Culture*
Partial shade.
Rich, moist, alkaline soil.
May bolt to seed if soil dries out.
Propagate by seed in mid to late spring.

A very vigorous plant to 1.2 m tall. It is suited to temperate climates, so much so that it has become a weed in some places. Feathery leaves have an aniseed flavour and can be added to savoury dishes or used as a garnish. Foliage is usually dried and crumbled before use. The strongly flavoured seeds are used in pickling.
A bronze-leaved variety is also available, *Foeniculum vulgare* 'Purpureum' (Bronze Fennel). It is a hardy perennial growing to 2 m tall. Will tolerate dry conditions. Leaves have an aniseed flavour which can be used in savoury dishes and salads.

**Feverfew** *Chrysanthemum Parthenium* Asteraceae or Compositae

*At a glance*
Origin: Southeast Europe.
Hardiness: Hardy; can become invasive.
Habit: Erect bushy, aromatic perennial to 1 m tall.
Growth rate: Rapid.

*Culture*
Adaptable to most soils.
Needs ample moisture.
Requires bright light.
Propagate by seed (plants readily self-seed).

A small daisy-flowering bush to 0.5 m tall. Plants produce large quantities of seed, often causing its rapid spread throughout the garden. Flowers are produced in the second year of growth. Leaves, although not pleasant to eat, have been documented as an effective cure for arthritis if a few are eaten daily for several months.

**Garlic**—See Allium

**Geraniums**—See Scented Geraniums

**Germander** *Teucrium Chamaedrys* Lamiaceae or Labiatae

*At a glance*
Origin: Europe, southwest Asia, West Mediterranean Islands.
Hardiness: Hardy.
Habit: Small rhizomatous shrub to 4.5 m tall.
Growth rate: Medium to fast.

*Culture*
Ordinary soils.
Prefers full sun.
Tolerates dry periods.
Often used as edging plants or small hedges.

Germander was commonly grown as a hedge plant during the Elizabethan period in England. It has also been used medicinally to treat gout and rheumatism. Unlike many of the other 'old world herbs', very little modern research has been done on germander. We know nothing about whether it has any toxic effects on the body. A dwarf form *Teucrium chamedrys* var. *Prostratum* is available.

**Ginkgo** *Ginkgo biloba* Ginkgoaceae

*At a glance*
Origin: Southeast China.
Hardiness: Hardy in temperate areas.
Habit: Large deciduous tree.
Growth rate: Slow when young

*Culture*
Temperate climate.
Full sun.
Deep, moist, fertile soil.
Propagate by seed, layering, cuttings or grafting.

Ginkgo is a hardy, pollution-tolerant, slow-growing tree. The yellow autumn leaves have been used as a medicinal tea to enhance memory. The kernels, known as gingko nuts, are commonly eaten in Asia. The male tree is normally grown because fruit from the female tree has a particularly unpleasant odour. Oil from the seeds can cause dermatitis. A number of cultivars are available offering different shaped or coloured leaves.

**Horseradish** *Armoracia rusticana* Brassicaceae or Cruciferae

*At a glance*
Origin: Southeast Europe.
Hardiness: Fairly hardy.
Habit: Spreading, deep-rooted perennial. Roots can be invasive.
Growth rate: Fast.

*Culture*
Best planted in a tub rather than in the soil.
Sunny position.
Well-drained soil.
Can tolerate dry conditions.
Leaves die down in winter in cold areas.
Propagate by root cuttings or division in spring.

A small perennial to 30 cm tall; commonly grown as an annual. It has large shiny green tooth-edged leaves and a large swollen root that is used as a condiment and digestive aid. It is also used to relieve sinus conditions and is known to be high in vitamin C and to contain an antibiotic substance.

**Hyssop** *Hyssopus officinalis* Lamiaceae or Labiatae

*At a glance*
Origin: Southern and eastern Europe.
Hardiness: Hardy in dry conditions.
Habit: Woody shrub to 60 cm tall; dies down in winter.
Growth rate: Fast during growing season.

*Culture*
Sunny warm site.
Well-drained, fertile, alkaline soil.
Trim after flowering and again in spring.
Can be clipped to a hedge.
Propagate by seeds, cuttings or division in spring.

An attractive perennial with aromatic leaves and blue, white or reddish flowers. A tea made from the leaves is said to be good for the respiratory system. Leaves can also be used to flavour casseroles and salads and the oil extracted from the foliage is used in perfumes and liqueurs. Hyssop plants are reputed to repel white butterflies and are planted as a companion to cabbages.

**Good King Henry** *Chenopodium Bonus-Henricus* Chenopodiaceae

*At a glance*
Origin: Europe.
Hardiness: Very hardy and adaptable.
Habit: Coarse weedy perennial.
Growth rate: Rapid during growing season.

*Culture*
Sunny to part shade.
Prefers well-drained soil.
Can become a weed due to hardiness and ease of growing.
Propagate by seed.

A plant to 80 cm tall with arrow-shaped leaves and long stems bearing small greenish flowers. The leaves can be used as a spinach substitute.

**Honeysuckle** *Lonicera* species Caprifoliaceae

*At a glance*
Number of species: 150.
Origin: East Asia.
Hardiness: Easy to grow.
Habit: Vigorous climbers or small bushy shrubs; some species are deciduous.
Growth rate: Rapid.

*Culture*
Sunny sites will produce the best floral displays but plants will flower in shady areas.
Well-drained, cool, moist, fertile soil is recommended.
Shelter is required from winds.
Pruning is necessary to control growth.
Many climbing species will readily produce roots from wherever the stem touches the ground.
Propagate by cuttings in spring and autumn.

*Herb species*
Common or Japanese Honeysuckle *Lonicera japonica*
Climber with vines up to 6 m long and cream-coloured, scented flowers in summer and autumn. Dried flowers are used in potpourris and scented pillows. The flowers are also an important ingredient in Chinese herbal medicine.

Perfoliate Honeysuckle *Lonicera Caprifolium*
Deciduous climber with reddish buds which open to soft pale yellow or cream flowers. Berries are poisonous.

**Winter Honeysuckle**  *Lonicera fragrantissima*
Woody shrub to 4 m tall bearing fragrant cream-white flowers in pairs. Flowers are used in potpourri.

**Giant Burmese Honeysuckle**  *Lonicera hildebrandiana*
Vigorous climber to 20 m bearing long scented tubular yellow flowers which become orange-coloured as they mature. Flowers are used in potpourri.

## Honeywort  *Cerinthe major*  Boraginaceae

*At a glance*
Origin: Mediterranean.
Hardiness: Sensitive to hot weather.
Habit: Small annual herb.
Growth rate: Rapid when the weather cools down.

*Culture*
Choose a site that provides winter sun and summer shade.
Well-drained fertile soil. Mulching will help retain moisture in soil.
Water in dry periods is essential.
Propagate by seed in autumn. Readily self-seeds.

Honeywort is a small herb to 40 cm with distinctive yellow and red tubular flowers surrounded by green. It is renowned as a bee attractant.

## Juniper  *Juniperus communis*  Cupressaceae

*At a glance*
Origin: North American, Eurasia.
Hardiness: Hardy but does best in temperate areas.
Habit: Large shrub or small tree.
Growth rate: Slow growing.

*Culture*
Prefers cool to cold environments
Prefers good drainage but needs a moist root run.
Bright light to full sun.

Juniper normally grows to 10 m tall although there are a number of forms in varying shapes, sizes and foliage colours. The ripe berries are used in some herbal medicines, however it should be noted these can be dangerous for pregnant women and people with kidney complaints. Berries only tend to appear in mild climates and they can take up to 3 years to ripen. Leaves can be added to a bath to create a rich scent which clears the sinuses and soothes aching muscles. Dried berries are also used to flavour gin.

## Jasmine  *Jasminum* species  Oleaceae

*At a glance*
Number of species: 200.
Origin: Asia, Africa and Australia.
Hardiness: Very hardy and adaptable plants.
Habit: Climbers.
Growth rate: Vigorous but slows down over winter.

*Culture*
Full sun to light shade.
Shelter from strong winds.
Rich organic soils will produce abundant growth.
Pruning may be needed to keep plant under control.
Propagate by seeds, layering or cuttings.

*Herb species*
Chinese jasmine  *Jasminum polyanthum*
A vigorous climber, with masses of attractive white flowers and deep pink or crimson buds in spring and summer. It prefers a moist but well-drained soil and can be pruned hard after flowering. The flowers are a valuable ingredient in potpourris. Native to western China.

White jasmine  *Jasminum officinale*
A white-flowering, highly scented climber to 9 m. Flowers are produced in summer. Can be slow growing if conditions are not perfect. Oil extracted from the flowers is used in perfumery. Native to western China through to the Himalayas.

## Lavender  *Lavandula* species  Lamiaceae or Labiatae

*At a glance*
Number of species: 20.
Origin: Mediterranean to India.
Hardiness: Hardy if provided with preferred growth requirements.
Habit: Small aromatic shrubs or herbs.
Growth rate: Growth can stop during winter months.

*Culture*
Full sun. Plants may need protection from sun in hot northern areas.
Requires perfect drainage. Provide raised beds if drainage is poor.
Tolerates very dry conditions.
Not very suitable in tropical districts.
Pruning may be needed to maintain shape. Do not prune below green growth.
Flowers can be eaten by grasshoppers and grubs. Remove grubs by hand.

Propagate by fresh heel cuttings in autumn or spring.

*Herb species*

English lavender  *Lavandula angustifolia*
A hardy perennial shrub, normally to 1 m tall, although there are many varieties of varying sizes. Leaves are linear-shaped to 5 cm long; whitish when young, turning to green as they mature. The flowers are mauve-coloured.
Dried flowers are used in potpourri and many scented crafts. Commercial oils are extracted from selected varieties for use in cosmetics.

French lavender (*Lavandula dentata*)

French lavender  *Lavandula dentata*
Perennial shrub growing between 30 cm and 1 m tall. The narrow grey-green leaves are 4 cm long with square, toothed edges. Short, soft-stemmed, plump spikes of dark lavender flowers are borne in the warmer months. The flowers have a strong lavender scent tinged with a light camphor fragrance. When dried the fragrance only lasts about 3–6 months. Unlike English lavender, this species will not tolerate cold conditions.

*Lavandula latifolia*
This species resembles English lavender although the leaves are greyer and more tomentose (hairy).

*Lavandula multifida*
Shrub to 70 cm tall with grey, tomentose leaves. Flowers are blue-violet.

*Lavandula pinnata*
Shrub to 1 m tall with pinnate leaves to 5 cm long. Lavender-coloured flowers.

Spanish lavender  *Lavandula stoechas*
Shrub to 1 m tall; leaves are 1–2.5 cm long, narrow and grey. Short spikes of dark purple flowers are borne in spring. The fragrance of the flowers is a blend of camphor and lavender with minty undertones.

Green lavender  *Lavandula viridis*
Sometimes considered to be a variety of *Lavandula stoechas*. Green lavender grows to 1 m tall and more than 1 m in diameter with sticky narrow green leaves and white flowers in a green head. It is a particularly hardy type of lavender although it is not suited to warm climates. The flowers have a strong lavender-pine scent. It can be easily grown from cuttings.

**Lamb's Ears or Betony**  *Stachys* species Lamiaceae or Labiatae

*At a glance*
Number of species: 300.
Origin: Europe.
Hardiness: Hardy.
Habit: Small perennial herbs and shrubs.
Growth rate: Fast during the growing season.

*Culture*
Sunny site.
Well-drained position. Can tolerate droughts.
Prune back to basal clump after flowering.
Propagate by cuttings or division.

*Herb species*

Lamb's Ears or Woolly Betony  *Stachys byzantina*
Creeping, furry grey-white stems and leaves, and pink-purple flowers. Hardy plant which adapts to most soils. Prefers full sun but will tolerate some shade. Can become invasive, taking root as it spreads.

Betony  *Stachys officinalis*
A mat-forming perennial with green leaves and erect rosy flower spikes up to 40 cm. A white flowering form is also available. Leaves are used for gastric and migraine disorders. A yellow dye can be extracted from the plant.

**Lavender Cotton**  *Santolina* species  Asteraceae or Compositae

*At a glance*
Number of species: Approximately 8.
Origin: Mediterranean.
Hardiness: Hardy.

Habit: Small shrubs.
Growth rate: Medium to fast.

*Culture*
Good drainage, tolerate dry periods.
Protect from severe frost. Mulch to insulate roots in cold climates.
Avoid extreme humidity.
Grow well as a hedge plant.
Propagates easily from cuttings.

*Herb species*
Lavender cotton  *Santolina Chamaecyparissus*
A small silver-grey woody shrub to 0.6 m tall. Hardy and drought resistant, preferring sun and good drainage, but highly adaptable, particularly in temperate climates. Tolerates dry salt infected soils.
Plants make an excellent small hedge or garden border. Dried flowers are used in potpourri. A dwarf form is also available.

*Santolina rosmarinifolia*
Spreading shrub to 0.6 m tall with fine blue-green foliage and yellow flowers.

Green santolina  *Santolina virens*
Spreading green shrub to 0.5 m tall with yellow flowers.

**Lemon grass**  *Cymbopogon citratus*  Poaceae or Gramineae

*At a glance*
Origin: Southern India and Sri Lanka.
Hardiness: Semi-hardy to very hardy in warm areas.
Habit: Clump-forming grass.
Growth rate: Rapid during warm months.

*Culture*
Full sun in a warm spot.
Well-drained soil. Can tolerate occasional drought.
Needs plenty of water in summer.
Protect from frosts and strong winds.
Leaves are susceptible to rust (fungus) problems in cool weather.
Propagate by division.

A grass to 1.8 m tall in warm climates but only grows to 1 m maximum in cooler temperate areas. (Lemon grass grows well in Sydney but needs protection from extreme cold in Melbourne.)
Leaves are a source of vitamin A and are used fresh or dry to make lemon grass tea. Oil is extracted from the leaves and used in perfumes. A closely-related species *Cymbopogon nardus*, grown mainly in Sri Lanka and South East Asia, is a major source of citronella oil.

**Lemon Verbena**  *Aloysia triphylla*  Verbenaceae

*At a glance*
Origin: Argentina and Chile.
Hardiness: Hardy.
Habit: Woody shrub.
Growth rate: Slows down or stops over winter.

*Culture*
Warm, sunny position.
Well-drained soil. Mulched in spring.
Tolerates dry conditions but prefers slightly moist soil.
Protect from frost.
Prune regularly to maintain shape.
Propagate by heel cuttings in summer.

A deciduous shrub in temperate climates, usually to 1.5 m tall (can grow to 3 m tall in warm areas). Does not like extreme cold or heat. Leaves are picked individually and used fresh or dry as a tea, in cooking as a lemon substitute, or in potpourri (leaves retain scent for a number of years). Used to relieve indigestion.

**Liquidamber**  *Liquidambar Styraciflua*  Hamamelidaceae

*At a glance*
Origin: Central America.
Hardiness: Hardy.
Habit: Deciduous tree.
Growth rate: Rapid growth during summer; dormant in winter.

*Culture*
Fertile, deep, moist soil.
Tolerates wet soil.
Full sun for best canopy spread.
Protect from strong winds.
Cool winters provides best autumn leaf diplay.
Roots can become invasive and damage pipe systems.
Propagate by seeds (seeds will be slow to germinate).

Also called sweet gum, liquidamber is a popular deciduous garden tree in cool and temperate climates. It will grow in the subtropics although autumn colours will not be as spectacular as plants grown in cooler areas. Growing 15–30 m tall, it prefers a deep, moist, fertile soil. The fragrant bark has been used in herbal medicines and perfumes.

**Lovage** *Levisticum officinale* Apiaceae or Umbelliferae

*At a glance*
Origin: Southern Europe.
Hardiness: Hardy.
Habit: Leafy perennial clump that dies down to the roots in winter.
Growth rate: Rapid in warm months.

*Culture*
Deep, moist soil.
Sun or partial shade.
Cut back flower stems in autumn.
Propagate by root division or seed in spring.

In temperate climates lovage can grow to 2 m tall. Leaves are used to flavour salads and savoury dishes. The root has been used as a tobacco substitute when chewed; a stimulant to the kidneys; and to relieve constipation. Leaves are picked while young, thin and tender, then dried. Roots are dug in late autumn of the second year, then washed, sliced and dried.

**Marigold** *Tagetes* species Asteraceae or Compositae

*At a glance*
Number of species: 30.
Origin: Mexico and Guatemala.
Hardiness: Very hardy.
Habit: Annual or perennials.
Growth rate: Rapid.

*Culture*
Full sun.
Well-drained soil.
Protect from frosts and strong winds.
Can tolerate hot dry weather but is best watered in dry conditions.
Removal of spent flowers will prolong flower period and prevent self-seeding.
Propagate by seed.

*Herb species*
French marigold *Tagetes patula*
A compact, bushy annual to 45 cm tall. Large orange flowers are produced in summer. Plant near tomatoes to control white fly.

Sweet marigold or Winter tarragon *Tagetes lucida*
A perennial to 50 cm tall with anise-flavoured leaves and small yellow flowers. In cold climates this plant may not recover after frosts or winter. Dried leaves are used to make a tea.

**Marjoram**—See Oregano

**Meadowsweet** *Spiraea Ulmaria* Rosaceae

*At a glance*
Origin: Northern Hemisphere.
Hardiness: Generally hardy.
Habit: Deciduous shrubs.
Growth rate: Medium to fast.

*Culture*
Adaptable to most soils but prefers fertile, moist soil.
Sunny or semi-shaded position.
Propagate by cuttings in late summer.

A medium-sized perennial with square, reddish stems and aromatic, serrated leaves which are dark green in colour on the topside of the leaf and white on the underside. The flowers are creamy-white, small and highly scented, appearing in spring and summer. The leaves are used to make an astringent-flavoured tea which is sometimes used as a remedy for diarrhoea in children.

**Melalaleuca or Tea tree** *Melaleuca alternifolia* Myrtaceae

*At a glance*
Origin: Eastern coast of Australia.
Hardiness: Very hardy.
Habit: Large bushy shrub.
Growth rate: Medium.

*Culture*
Full sun but can tolerate heavy shade.
Adaptable to many soils except very dry situations.
Good plant for poorly drained sites.

Woody shrub, 5–6 m tall with papery bark and narrow leaves to 2.5 cm. Small white bottlebrush flowers appear in summer. This species occurs naturally in coastal areas of northern and central NSW. The northern varieties contain cineol: a component in the oil which has a number of valuable properties used in medicinal therapies. The oil is used as an antiseptic, a mild anaesthetic (for relief of arthritic pain), an inhalant for relief of colds, and to repel insects. The cineol content can vary from 6 to 16% of the total oil and if plants are grown commercially it is essential to select a variety with high cineol content.

# Mint   *Mentha* species   Lamiaceae or Labiatae

*At a glance*
Number of species: 25.
Natural habitat: Temperate regions throughout the world.
Hardiness: Hardy if supplied with preferred growing requirements.
Habit: Low-growing perennial herbs.
Growth rate: Rapid.

*Culture*
Full sun.
Moist soil is essential.
Shaded position only if plant cannot be kept moist.
Susceptible to rust in cooler months.
Keep under control by planting in a separate garden bed or container.
Propagate by cuttings, division or seed.

*Herb species*
Water mint   *Mentha aquatica*
Strongly scented plant to 1 m tall with well branched stems. Purple flowers appear in late summer. *Mentha aquatica* var. *crispa* is the most popular variety for flavouring food and is one of the best mints for digestive treatments.

Field mint   *Mentha arvensis*
Erect hairy plant, growing between 30 and 70 cm tall. Lilac, white or (rarely) pink flowers appear in summer. Important as a commercial source of menthol in Japan.

Lemon or Orange mint   *Mentha citrata*
Lemon mint is actually a variety of peppermint, *Mentha × piperita* var. *citrata*. The foliage has a strong citrus-mint scent. The flavour is usually considered too strong for eating. The dried foliage or extracted oil is used in potpourri.

Lemon mint (*Mentha citrata*)

Common mint   *Mentha cordifolia*
Suckering and clump-forming mint to 0.5 m tall. It thrives in moist soil and prefers filtered sun. In a warm position leaves will continue to grow throughout winter. Leaves are very commonly used in cooking to make mint sauce or jelly, added to drinks or desserts, mixed in potato salad or with cooked peas, etc.

Horse mint   *Mentha longifolia*
Variable hairy white or grey mint growing between 30 cm and 1 m tall, often purple tinged. Lilac or white flowers appear in summer. Many hybrid varieties.

Peppermint   *Mentha × piperita = M. aquatica × M. spicata*
Grows to 1 m tall over summer but will die back to ground level in cooler climates over winter. Foliage is often purple tinged. Lilac pink flowers are borne in summer.
Excellent as a repellent for insects or rodents. Used for flavouring in cooking and confectionary or drunk as a hot tea. An important ingredient in many herbal medicines.

Pennyroyal   *Mentha Pulegium*
Creeping plant to 30 cm tall with dense lilac flowers in summer. Plants can be grown as a herb lawn. The leaves are used as an insect repellant (particularly effective on ants) and as a tea to soothe the stomach. The strong oils in the foliage can have negative effects and pennyroyal tea should not be taken by pregnant women.

Pennyroyal (*Mentha Pulegium*)

Corsican mint   *Mentha Requienii*
Creeping mint with tiny tender leaves and blue-pink summer flowers. Corsican mint is more tender than other herbs and will die off and rot in patches if the soil is too wet or dry. A strong scent is released when bruised and is ideally suited to planting between stepping stones or beside paving.

Apple mint   *Mentha suaveolens*
Hairy grey-green or golden variegated foliage. Plants grow to 1 m tall in spring, but die back to the roots

over winter. Whitish or pink flowers appear in summer. A very hardy plant in moist soils—in some localities in can become an invasive weed.

Leaves are used fresh as a garnish or to flavour drinks and food. Leaves may be dried and used in potpourri. Apple mint is sometimes incorrectly classified as *M. rotundifolia* which is actually *M. longifolia* × *M. suaveolens*.

**Spearmint** *Mentha spicata* (*M. spicata* = *M. viridis*) Similar to peppermint in requirements and growth habit, only differing in flavour and leaf colour. An important culinary herb, particularly used for flavouring drinks and sweets.

**Curly mint** *Mentha spicata* 'Crispata'
A rapid growing plant to 60 cm tall with hairy stems and wrinkled, broad, dull green leaves. Pale purple flowers are borne on spikes. This is a very aromatic mint. Oils can be used as antiseptics or as a condiment. The leaves can be dried for potpourri or eaten fresh in salads, as a digestive aid or in a refreshing mint tea or tonic.

*Commercial Production*
Production of mint oil has a long history: the ancient Egyptians are known to have distilled oil from peppermint. *Mentha arvensis*, *M. piperita* and *M. spicata* are grown commercially in the USA; current production is around 1000 metric tonnes annually, mainly on moist soils on the northwest coastal states of Oregon and Washington.

Typically spearmint and peppermint are planted as rhizomes in rows. Weeds are controlled by cultivation in the first year. In late autumn, the plants are ploughed in before the first frost. The underground rhizomes spread rapidly and reappear the following season. The leaves are cut with a mower and left to dry until the moisture content drops to approximately 35% at which point it is collected and distilled for oil using steam distillation.

**Mint bush** *Prostanthera* species Lamiaceae or Labiatae

*At a glance*
Number of species: Approximately 65.
Origin: Australia.
Hardiness: Moderately hardy.
Habit: Small or medium shrubs.
Growth rate: Generally fast.

*Culture*
Provide some protection from full sun and wind.

Water over dry months.
Most species are drought tolerant and tolerate light frosts.
Highly susceptible to cinnamon fungus. In affected areas plants must be grafted onto *Westringia* rootstock.
Generally propagate by softwood cuttings.

*Herb species*
The following species have scented foliage:

*Prostanthera cineolifera*
A shrub to 2 m tall with mauve flowers in spring.

*Prostanthera cuneata*
A small, rounded shrub to 0.5 m tall and 1 m diameter. White-mauve flowers are borne in summer.

*Prostanthera incisa*
Grows to 1.5 m tall; toothed leaves and violet-coloured flowers.

*Prostanthera melissifolia*
A medium-sized shrub, growing to 3 m tall and 3 m diameter. Pink or purple flowers are borne in spring.

*Prostanthera ovalifolia*
A popular garden shrub, growing to 3 m tall and 3 m diameter. Purple flowers are borne in spring.

*Prostanthera sieberi*
A rounded shrub to 1.5 m tall. Purple flowers are borne in spring.

**Mugwort**—See Artemisia

**Mulberry** *Morus nigra* Moraceae

*At a glance*
Origin: Western Asia.
Hardiness: Hardy.
Habit: Deciduous tree.
Growth rate: Fast growing during summer; dormant in winter.

*Culture*
Prefers full sun and rich, well-drained soil.
Tolerates short periods of waterlogging.
May be attacked by grasshoppers and the commercial 'silk worm'.
Maintenance required in cleaning up fruit stains.
Propagate by seed or grafting.

Tree to 9 m tall with deep purple to black fruit. Bark and fruits have a laxative effect when ingested. Berries are also said to help reduce fever.

**Mullein**  *Verbascum* species   Scrophulariaceae

*At a glance*
Number of species: Approximately 250.
Origin: Mediterranean.
Hardiness: Hardy to very hardy in temperate climates.
Habit: Herbaceous clump.
Growth rate: Fast.

*Culture*
Adapted to most soils.
Avoid waterlogging, extreme cold and high humidity.
Propagate by cuttings, seed or division.

*Herb species*
Woolly mullein  *Verbascum bombyceferum*
Felt-like leaves, flower spike to 2 m tall, often branched with yellow flowers.

*Verbascum chaixii*
Mildly toothed green to grey green leaves, white flowers on spikes to 1 m tall. Plants often self-seed and may become a weed.

Purple mullein  *Verbascum phoeniceum*
Dark green lower leaves, flower spikes with finer leaves and flowers which can vary in colour according to variety.
Muellin varieties are now grown as ornamental plants, though they have been used in the past as a medicinal herb.

**Myrtle**  *Myrtus communis*   Myrtaccac

*At a glance*
Origin: Mediterranean region and southwest Europe.
Hardiness: Hardy.
Habit: Shrub or small tree.
Growth rate: Medium to fast.

*Culture*
Prefers full sun and rich, well-drained soil.
Protect from wind and frost.
Propagate by cuttings in spring.

Rounded small tree or shrub to 5 m tall with dense, shiny dark green, scented leaves and white, fragrant flowers in summer. There are dwarf, variegated and double flower forms available in nurseries. Dried flower buds and fruit have been crushed and used as a spice. Dried flowers and leaves can be used in potpourri.

**Nasturtium**  *Tropaeolum* species   Tropaeolaceae

There are two genera: *Nasturtium* (watercress), and *Tropaeolum*, which is given the common name 'nasturtium'.

*At a glance*
Number of species: Over 50.
Origins: Mountains of central America through to South America.
Hardiness: Very hardy.
Habit: Spreading or climbing annual or perennial herbs.
Growth rate: Generally fast.

*Culture*
Adapted to most soils, but prefers moist or even wet soil.
Responds to feeding.
Propagate by seed, usually early spring, or autumn in hot climates.

*Herb species*
Nasturtium  *Tropaeolum majus*
Although it is more often grown as an annual flower, the common nasturtium is a versatile creeping herb. The flowers are edible and can be mixed into salads or used as a garnish. Nasturtium is also a popular companion plant, helping to control insects (particularly aphis) on adjacent plants.

*Tropaeolum tuberosum*
A vigorous climber which produces large, long, edible underground tubers.

**Oregano and Marjoram**  *Origanum* species   Lamiaceae or Labiatae

*At a glance*
Number of species: Up to 20.
Origin: Europe (mainly the Mediterranean).
Hardiness: Hardy.
Habit: Small, occasionally creeping shrubs.
Growth rate: Fast.

*Culture*
Prefers well-drained soil.
Responds to watering in dry hot conditions.
Responds to feeding.
Regular pruning is essential to encourage lush growth (which is best for harvesting).
Propagate by cuttings or layering. Creeping varieties are also be propagated by division.

### Herb species

**Sweet marjoram** *Origanum Marjorana*
A warm weather plant, to 30 cm tall with yellow to grey-green leaves and tiny white flowers. In cold climates, marjoram is often grown as an annual; the seed is sown in early spring. A popular culinary herb, marjoram has a sweeter flavour than other origanums.

**Pot marjoram** *Origanum Onites*
A shrub to 0.5 m tall with finer and more wiry stems than other origanums. The leaves are pale green, flowers are pink.

**Golden marjoram** *Origanum vulgare* 'Aureum'
A clump forming plant to 0.4 m tall with creeping (suckering) stems, golden-green foliage and pink flowers.

**Wild marjoram** *Origanum vulgare*
A semi-hardy, frost tender perennial to 0.2 m tall. Grows best in a warm, sunny position in well-drained, fertile soil. Leaves are used fresh or dried in savoury dishes—particularly pasta, meats and vegetables. Closely related to oregano.

**Oregano** *Origanum vulgare* 'Viride'
Grows to 0.6 m tall with pale to white-green, slightly hairy leaves. Oregano leaves can be eaten fresh or dried and the flowers can produce a reddish-brown to purple dye that is not very durable. Oregano should be pruned before flowering to maintain shape. It is propagated by seed, cuttings or root division.

## Orris Root *Iris* × *germanica* var. florentina Iridaceae

*At a glance*
Origin: Europe
Hardiness: Generally hardy.
Habit: Clump-forming perennials.
Growth rate: Fast in moist, fertile soils.

*Culture*
Prefers well-drained but moist soil.
Responds to feeding.
Remove dead flowers and foliage as plants die back seasonally.
Propagate by division.

Orris root powder is obtained from the underground rhizomes (roots). The rhizomes are lifted during winter while the plants are dormant. They are then peeled, chopped, dried and ground into a fine powder for use in potpourri. Orris root powder is a fixative, helping the scents of other plants remain in the potpourri for a longer period.

## Parsley *Petroselinum crispum* Apiaceae or Umbelliferae

*At a glance*
Origin: Europe and western Asia.
Hardiness: Hardy.
Habit: Annual or biennial clump.
Growth rate: Very fast.

*Culture*
Full sunlight.
Good drainage.
Fertile or well fertilised soil.
Avoid excessive wet or dry soils.
Propagate by seed in spring (cool climates) or autumn (hot climates). Seed is often started in a greenhouse because it can be slow to germinate.

*Herb varieties*
*Petroselinum crispum* is the only species cultivated, though it has been known under a variety of other names including *P. hortense, P. tuberosum* and *P. sativum*. There is a number of varieties of *P. crispum*; the two most popular are curled parsley and Italian parsley.

**Curled parsley** *Petroselinum crispum* var. crispum
Parsley normally lives for two seasons. In temperate climates it prefers a sunny, moist position and responds to regular feeding and good drainage. In warmer climates plants should be grown in indirect sunlight and mulch applied around the roots. Parsley is an excellent plant to grow in a large pot providing a good quality potting mix is used and the plants are regularly fed.
Leaves are used as a garnish or chopped and added to cooked foods at the end of the cooking process—too much heat destroys the flavour. Harvest leaves by pulling them downwards off the central stem, removing the complete leaf stalk.

**Italian or Plain Leaf Parsley** *Petroselinum crispum* var. neopolitanum
This variety has a stronger flavoured foliage and is favoured by chefs. As with any parsley, it is rich in vitamin A and C, and has a variety of medicinal uses (parsley should not be over-eaten during pregnancy though).

**Hamburg or Turnip rooted parsley** *Petroselinum*

*crispum* var. tuberosum
A less common variety with an enlarged edible root.

## Rose  *Rosa* species  Rosaceae

*At a glance*
Number of species: Around 100 species and more than 20,000 cultivars; many being hybrids.
Origin: Europe and Asia.
Hardiness: Hardy to very hardy.
Habit: Low to tall shrubs and climbers.
Growth rate: Medium to fast.

*Culture*
Fertile and well-drained but moist soil. In heavy (i.e. clay) soils, plant roses on a mound to improve drainage. In light soils and warm climates mulching is needed to keep the roots moist and cool over summer. Regular feeding is essential. They will respond to generous annual applications of well-rotted manure. Full or filtered sun.
Most roses are hardy and will grow in a wide range of climates including cold (snow-prone) areas to warm sub-tropical climates.
Flowering is improved by annual pruning. In cool climates they are normally pruned very hard during winter (removing more than 70%). In warm climates, pruning should be light (10–20% annually), a couple of times each year.
Aphis, black spot and some other problems need to be controlled. Disease is reduced by planting in a sunny, airy position. Avoid planting near doorways, paths, walls, or too close to other plants. Plant garlic at the base of roses to deter black spot and aphis. Heavy infestations of aphis can be controlled naturally with pyrethrum spray or soapy water (ie. throw the wash water over the bush).
Propagate by cuttings, budding or grafting.
Some rose species are important sources of oils for perfumes. Rose petals are widely used in potpourri. Rose hips are an excellent source of vitamin C.

*Herb varieties*
In general, all old-fashioned 'Musk roses' are scented. There are both scented and non-scented varieties amongst the hybrid teas, floribundas, climbers and miniatures.

*Hybrid Teas*
These are the best for cut flowers, producing large, well formed flowers on strong stems. The plants are generally less attractive, more woody and taller than the floribundas. These hybrid tea varieties are scented:

| | | |
|---|---|---|
| Adolf Horstman | Mister Lincoln | Red Lion |
| Baronne de | My Choice | Shot Silk |
| Rothschild | Ophelia | Silver Lining |
| Bettina | Papa Meilland | Sutter's Gold |
| Blue Moon | Paradise | Tenerife |
| Champion | Peace | Troika |
| Crimson Glory | Pink Peace | Typhoo Tea |
| Dekorat | Queen | Typhoon |
| Dutch Gold | Elizabeth | Wendy Cussons |
| Ena Harkness | Red Star | Whisky Mac |
| Ernest H. | Prima Ballerina | |
| Morse | Red Devil | |

*Floribundas*
Compared to hybrid teas, floribundas are smaller and bushier plants, with larger bunches of smaller flowers occurring for longer periods. Scented hybrid teas include:

| | | |
|---|---|---|
| Apricot Nectar | Margaret Merril | Scented Air |
| Arthur Bell | Orange | Scherzo |
| Fragrant | Sensation | Woburn Abbey |
| Delight | Pernille Poulsen | Yesterday |
| Golden Slippers | Pineapple Doll | |
| Lili Marlene | Rosemary Rose | |

*Miniatures*
The following miniature roses are scented:

| | | |
|---|---|---|
| Baby Faurax | Lavender Lace | Rise 'n' shine |
| Baby | Little Flirt | Sweet Fairy |
| Masquerade | Magic Carousel | Yellow Doll |

*Climbers*
The following climbing roses are fragrant:

| | | |
|---|---|---|
| Albertine | Golden | Rosy Mantle |
| Aloha | Showers | Shot Silk |
| Compassion | Guinee | climber |
| Copenhagen | Maigold | Sympathie |
| Crimson Glory | Mermaid | The Garland |
| climber | Mme Alfred | Zephrine |
| Ena Harkness | Carriere | Drouhin |
| climber | Mme Gregoire | |
| Etiole De Hol- | Staechelin | |
| lande climber | New Dawn | |

*Fragrant foliage*
*Rosa eglanteria* (syn *R. rubiginosa*) is an exceptional rose having fragrant apple-scented foliage. Although attractive, the flowers only occur for a short time in summer. As such, it is grown more for the dark green scented leaves which can be dried and added to potpourri.

**Rosemary** *Rosmarinus officinalis* Lamiaceae or Labiatae

*At a glance*
Origin: Mediterranean region.
Hardiness: Medium.
Habit: Small woody shrubs.
Growth rate: Medium.

*Culture*
Prefers full sun.
Requires sandy but fertile soil.
Tolerates very cold temperatures, but may not tolerate excessive heat.
Propagates easily, but sometimes slowly, from cuttings.

*Herb varieties*
Rosemary *Rosmarinus officinalis*
Rosemary is a woody shrub to 1 m tall. Leaves are used fresh or dried in cooking, e.g. meats and vegetables, in herb butters, vinegars and jams. Rosemary oil, used in perfumery, is mainly produced in Spain and Tunisia.

Prostrate rosemary *Rosmarinus officinalis* 'Prostratus'
Low-growing form of rosemary to 0.3 m tall and 1 m diameter. Leaves are shorter and narrower than standard rosemary; flowers are pale blue. Requires a well-drained and not overly shaded position.

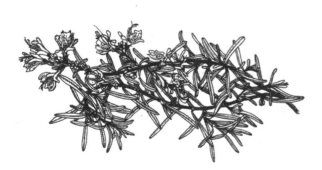

Prostrate rosemary (*Rosmarinus officinalis* 'Prostrata')

*Rosmarinus officinalis* 'Blue Lagoon'
A vigorous cultivar with deep rich blue flowers.

**Rue** *Ruta* species    Rutaceae

*At a glance*
Number of species: Approximately 40.
Natural habitat: Mediterranean and western Asia.
Hardiness: Hardy.
Habit: Low shrubs and herbs.
Growth rate: Fast.

*Culture*
Full or filtered sunlight.
Well-drained to dry, acidic soil.
Protect from strong winds and severe frost.
Prune to shape after flowering.
Propagate by seed in spring (cool climates) or autumn (hot climates).

*Herb varieties*
Rue *Ruta graveolens*
A perennial plant to 0.5 m tall with attractive grey green, lacy leaves. Traditionally used as a medicinal herb, rue can be dangerous if taken in large doses. Rue is used mainly fresh, but can be dried. The dried seed heads are attractive in flower arrangements. It is a popular companion plant though evidence to support its effectiveness is not as strong as many other companion plants.

Mountain rue *Ruta montana*
Finer, more lacy foliage than *Ruta graveolens*; greenish-yellow flowers; grows to 0.5 m tall.

**Sage** *Salvia* species    Lamiaceae or Labiatae

*At a glance*
Number of species: Over 750.
Origin: Europe, North and South America
Hardiness: Generally hardy.
Habit: Varied; low to tall shrubs.
Growth rate: Medium to very fast.

*Culture*
Full or lightly filtered sun.
Avoid waterlogged soils.
Prefer fertile, moist but well-drained soil.
Tolerate dry periods once established.
Prune hard after flowering to rejuvenate plant. Only one cut should be done in the first year, but two or three prunings can be done in subsequent years.
Plants become increasingly woody over the years, and are usually replaced after 5 to 6 years.
Propagate by seed, cuttings or division.

Honeysuckle (*Lonicera japonica*)

Honeywort

Horseradish (*Armoracia rusticana*)

Jasmine (*Jasmine polyanthum*)

*Iris germanica*

Lamb's ears (*Stachys byzantina*)

Italian lavender hedge

Green lavender (*Lavandula viridis*)

Lavender hedge
Lemon balm (*Melissa officinalis*)

Lemon grass (*Cymbopogon citratus*)
Lemon verbena (*Aloysia triphylla*)

*Herb species*
Blue sage  *Salvia clevelandii*
Shrub to 0.8 m tall with grey-green elliptic/oblong leaves to 3 cm long. Blue flowers form in heads at the end of branches. Native to western North America, blue sage requires full sun and excellent drainage. Virtually no watering should be done over summer once it is established. Leaves can be substituted in cooking for *Salvia officinalis*.

Pineapple-scented sage  *Salvia elegans*
A shrub to 1 m tall with soft, light green foliage to 3 cm long and red/scarlet flowers to 4 cm long, Plants are suckering and sometimes invasive. Dried flowers and leaves are used in potpourri. Leaves are used as a pineapple flavouring in cooking.

Mexican sage  *Salvia leucantha*
Very hardy and long-lived sage to 1.5 m tall with white woolly stems, narrow leaves and purple velvet-like flowers. Tolerates semi-shade and periods of dryness. Requires annual pruning to maintain a compact shape. Flowers are harvested and dried when just opening for use in potpourri or dry arrangements.

Common or garden sage  *Salvia officinalis*
A woody perennial shrub to 0.7 m tall in ideal conditions, although often smaller. Oblong leaves are between 2 and 6 cm; flowers are violet blue, pink or white. Susceptible to extremes of cold, heat, wind or moisture, sage prefers full sun and a well-drained but moist soil. Once established, sage is drought tolerant. Propagate by seed or cuttings.
Leaves are used in cooking, dried or fresh, to flavour meats, vegetables, butters, vinegars, etc. Extracted oil is used in perfumes. Several varieties are available, some with variegated or coloured foliage.

Dalmation white sage  *Salvia officinalis* var. Dalmatia
Grown commercially in the USA as a spice for flavouring sausages, soups and canned foods. Fresh leaves are used in herb vinegars, cheeses, liqueurs and pickles, and the oil is used in mouthwashes, gargles and perfumery. Although Dalmation white sage can be grown from seed, commercial plantings are established from cuttings of selected varieties. Cuttings are planted in spring after the frosts have finished. A low nitrogen soil produces the best oil percentages in the leaf, hence high phosphorus and potassium fertilisers are generally preferred. Harvesting should be done when there are no flowers present and the cut foliage can be left to partially sun dry. It is possible to harvest two or three times each season.

Purple-leaved sage  *Salvia officinalis* 'Purpurea'
Grows to 0.7 m tall with dark purple leaves and light mauve flowers. Purple-leaved sage is often not as hardy as the standard form of *Salvia officinalis* and plants may die partly or fully over a cold winter. Leaves can be used in cooking and are particularly useful as garnishes due to the unique colour.

Variegated sage  *Salvia officinalis* 'Variegata'
Golden variegated leaf form; slightly smaller and less vigorous than other forms of *Salvia officinalis*.

Clary sage  *Salvias Sclarea*
Upright growing biennial or perennial plant to 0.8 m tall, leaves are a broad ovate shape up to 20 cm long. Dried leaves can be used as a fixative in potpourri. Extracted oil is used both in cooking and in medicines.

**Santolina**—See Lavender Cotton

**Savory**  *Satureja* species  Lamiaceae or Labiatae

*At a glance*
Number of species: Approximately 30.
Origin: Mediterannean, southern Europe.
Hardiness: Medium to hardy.
Habit: Low or spreading shrubs.
Growth rate: Medium to fast.

*Culture*
Moist, fertile soil.
Full or filtered sun.
Watering is necessary over dry periods.
Propagate by division, cuttings or seed sown directly into final position.

*Herb species*
Summer savory  *Satureja hortensis*
An annual to 0.45 m tall; prefers full sun and a well-drained, rich organic soil. Propagate by seed. Leaves are used for their peppery flavour, particularly with meats and vegetables. To harvest, cut at ground level when flowering starts, and treat like mint.

Winter savory  *Satureja montana*
Dense shrub to 0.5 m tall with clusters of pink or white flowers. Leaves are used to flavour bean or meat dishes. Dried leaves have been eaten to aid digestion. Cutting stimulates growth, so harvest normally twice or more each year.

**Scented Geraniums** *Pelargonium and Geranium* species  Geraniaceae

Note: The majority of plants that are commonly called geraniums are in fact pelargoniums. (The common name of true geraniums is 'cranesbill'.) The main difference between these two closely related genera is the size of the petals: pelargoniums have two petals larger than the other three while geranium petals are the same size.

*At a glance*
Number of species: Approximately 280 pelargonium species.
Origin: Varies but most species are from South Africa.
Hardiness: Generally hardy.
Habit: Low to medium shrubs.
Growth rate: Generally fast.

*Culture*
Prefer full or filtered sunlight, tolerate some shade.
Prefer moist, fertile soil but many tolerate poorer conditions.
Protect from frost.
Prune hard after danger of cold weather.
Propagate by cuttings any time of the year.

*Herb species*
Scented geraniums are fascinating herbs, offering hundreds of different types with scents varying from lemon or mint to nutmeg or coconut. They cross-breed readily, and classification is incomplete and varies according to which source you refer to.
Scented pelargoniums and geraniums are edible and can be used in cooking to flavour various foods, including cakes, biscuits, confectionary and sweets. They are also valuable in herb crafts.

Rose-scented geranium  *Pelargonium capitatum*
Shrub to 0.6 m tall with pink flowers and spreading foliage covered with white hairs.

Lemon-scented pelargonium  *Pelargonium crispum*
Green-leaved form grows 0.5 to 0.9 m tall; the yellow variegated leaf form is much smaller. Leaves are small, stiff and crinkled; flowers are pale mauve or purple. The leaves have a strong lemon scent. Plants do well in full sun and make an excellent small hedge plant.

Rose-scented pelargonium  *Pelargonium graveolens*
Shrub to 1 m tall (less likely to spread than other pelargoniums) with grey-green foliage and tiny rose-pink flowers. Grows in semi-shade to full shade. Plants are grown commercially to produce 'geranoil'.

Coconut pelargonium  *Pelargonium grossularioides*
Spreading low shrub to 20 cm tall with reddish stems and small rich pink flowers. Grows in sun or shade and tolerates wet soils.

Lime-scented pelargonium  *Pelargonium* × *nervosum*
A light green upright bush to 1 m or more tall with small, richly lime-scented, crinkled leaves and white flowers. Plants grow well as a topiary standard.

Apple-scented pelargonium  *Pelargonium odoratissimum*
Spreading plant to 0.7 m tall with soft, green, apple-scented foliage and white flowers with red streaks. Grows best in full sun but tolerates some shade.

Oak leaf or cinnamon geranium  *Pelargonium quercifolium*
A sprawling shrub to 2 m wide with hairy rough leaves and pink-white flowers. Foliage can develop reddish tones in cold weather.

Rose-scented pelargonium  *Pelargonium radens*
Upright shrub to 1 m tall with deeply divided leaves and small pink flowers. Perhaps the best of the rose-scented species.

Peppermint-scented geranium  *Pelargonium tomentosum*
A low, soft, grey-green shrub to 2 m diameter and 1.5 m tall. The white flowers are streaked with red. Grows best in filtered sunlight or shade; avoid humid climates and frost.

Herb robert  *Geranium robertianum*
Clump-forming annual to 20 cm tall and 40 cm diameter. Stems and sometimes leaves can develop tones of red; flowers are pink. Plants self-seed readily, often becoming a weed (but an attractive one). The dried plant is used in some herbal medicines.

**Southernwood**—See Artemisia

**Sorrel or Dock**  *Rumex* species  Polygonaceae

*At a glance*
Number of species: Over 100.
Origin: Europe.
Hardiness: Very hardy.

Habit: Creeping or clump-forming weeds; many species are weeds.
Growth rate: Rapid.

*Culture*
Shade or filtered sunlight.
Can be invasive, so best grown in a tub or confined garden bed and not allowed to flower.
Prefer moist soil.
Tolerate poor conditions.
Propagate by seed or (for creeping types) division.

*Herb species*
Garden sorrel  *Rumex Acetosa*
A hardy, creeping plant to 0.5 m or more tall, which can become a weed if left uncontrolled. Grows best in semi-shade and a fertile, moist soil. Propagate by division in spring.
Leaves have both culinary and medicinal uses.

French sorrel  *Rumex scutatus*
Forms a spreading clump to 0.5 m tall (often less) with green flowers which change to a pink-red colour. The edible leaves have a sour lemon flavour.

## Soapwort  *Saponaria* species  Caryophyllaceae

*At a glance*
Number of species: Approximately 30.
Origin: Mainly Mediterranean.
Hardiness: Hardy.
Habit: Annual, biennial or perennial herbs.
Growth rate: Fast.

*Culture*
Tolerates poor soils and shade.
Prefers good drainage.
Some species can become weeds.
Water in dry weather.
Prune old flower heads once they start to die.
Propagate by seed or (some types) by division.

*Herb species*
Soapwort  *Saponaria officinalis*
A small, spreading plant to 0.5 m tall with pink scented flowers in summer and autumn. Foliage dies back to roots over cold weather and regrows in spring. In the past, leaves were used for washing the body and made into a tea for washing clothes.

Prostrate soapwort  *Saponaria Ocymoides*
Creeping plant to 0.2 m tall with sweet-scented purple-pink flowers. This plant often dies after flowering.

## Strawberry  *Fragaria* species  Rosaceae

*At a glance*
Number of species: Approximately 12.
Natural habitat: Europe.
Hardiness: Hardy.
Habit: Clumping herb.
Growth rate: Fast.

*Culture*
Requires good drainage, moist and fertile soil.
Fruit needs protection from birds, slugs and other pests.
Weed control is essential.
Virus diseases carried by aphis can be devastating.
Propagate from runners taken from virus-free plants.

*Herb varieties*
Alpine strawberry  *Fragaria vesca* 'Semperflorens'
A small perennial to 0.2 m tall with small serrated leaves and small but very tasty strawberry fruits during warm weather. Needs moist, fertile soil to do best. Prefers filtered but bright light. Ideal as a border plant.

*Commercial varieties*
A wide range of large fruiting commercial varieties are grown today. These are generally less hardy than the alpine strawberry, but they do give heavier fruit crops.

## Tansy  *Tanacetum vulgare*  Asteraceae or Compositae

*At a glance*
Origin: Europe and Asia.
Hardiness: Hardy to very hardy.
Habit: Small clumps or shrubs.
Growth rate: Fast.

Tansy (*Tanacetum vulgare*)

*Culture*
Avoid wet soils.
Tolerates poorer soils but grows better if fed.
Propagate by seed or division
A clump-forming herb to 1 m tall, dying back to the roots in winter before regrowing in spring. Very

hardy, although grows best in a well-drained, fertile soil. It can become invasive, although not as bad as some herbs. Flowers can be dried for decoration or potpourri. Foliage can be used as an insect repellant. Do not take internally.

A 'crinkled' leaf variety, *Tanacetum vulgare* 'crispum', is often grown for its more attractive appearance.


**Tarragon—See Artemisia**


**Thyme**   *Thymus* species   Labiatae or Lamiaceae

*At a glance*
Number of species: Up to 400.
Origin: Varied, mainly Europe and western Asia.
Hardiness: Generally hardy once established.
Habit: Low shrubs or creepers, usually woody.
Growth rate: Medium.

*Culture*
Requires moist soil; extremes of wet or dry are best avoided.
Prefers full or filtered sunlight.
Propagate by cuttings or division.
Harvest when flowering and air dry. Flowers and leaves can be powdered or chopped. Discard coarse stems. Two or three harvests in a season can normally be made.

*Herb species*
*Thymus caespititius*
Prostrate, mat-forming herb with flower stems to 1.5–3 cm tall. Hairy leaves are borne in dense tufts to 1 cm long. Flowers are purplish-pink to white.

*Thymus camphoratus*
Small shrub 10–25 cm tall, leaves 2–4 mm long, white underneath. Purple to rose-coloured flowers about 1 cm long.

Variegated lemon thyme   *Thymus citriodorus* 'Aureus' (*Thymus citriodorus = T. pulegioides ×* *T. vulgaris*)
Small shrub to 30 cm tall with pink flowers and variegated leaves. Leaves are used fresh or dry to add lemon flavour to fish, meats and vegetables. Can be shorter-lived than some other thymes.

Caraway thyme   *Thymus Herba-barona*
Small shrub, 4–10 cm tall, with rose-coloured flowers. Foliage has a caraway scent when crushed.

*Thymus praecox*
Small creeping shrub with long and woody stems, leathery leaves and purple flowers.

*Thymus pulegioides*
Spreading bushy shrub to 8–25 cm tall with mauve flowers.

Lemon thyme   *Thymus Serpyllum*
Mat-forming shrub; roots form at stem nodes. Purple flowers stand erect to 8 cm tall.

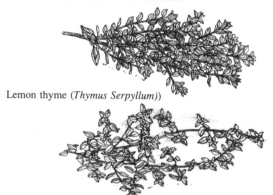

Lemon thyme (*Thymus Serpyllum*))

Garden thyme (*Thymus vulgaris*)

Common or garden thyme   *Thymus vulgaris*
A low-growing woody plant to 30 cm tall, bearing large numbers of white to lilac flowers. Prefers indirect sun, and a well-drained but moist soil (responds to mulching). Plants are relatively hardy once established. Water regularly in warm weather. Propagated by cuttings or division.
Leaves are used in vinegars, herb butters, herbal teas or to flavour meat and vegetable dishes.

**Vietnamese or Hot Mint**   *Polygonum odoratum*   Polygonaceae

*At a glance*
Origin: Asia.
Hardiness: Hardy in moist soil.
Habit: Creeping herb.
Growth rate: Fast.

*Culture*
Requires moist, fertile soil.
Prefers full sun.
Often grown in a tub to prevent it becoming a weed.

A vigorous, creeping plant to 0.5 m tall, with small pink flowers in summer. Leaves are used to give a hot spiced flavour to meats, rice and vegetables. Also called Indonesian mint or rau ram.

**Violet**  *Viola odorata*  Violaceae

*At a glance*
Origin: Europe.
Hardiness: Medium to hardy.
Habit: Creeping or clump-forming ground covers.
Growth rate: Medium to fast.

*Culture*
Prefers filtered sunlight or part shade, but can take full sun in colder temperate climates.
Protected from extreme heat.
Moist to wet, fertile soil.
Avoid waterlogging or extreme dryness.
Propagate by division or occasionally seed.

A small, perennial, clump-forming plant to 0.2 m tall, with strongly perfumed blue-violet flowers in late winter. Oil is used in perfumery; flowers are used in potpourri.

**Wormwood**—See Artemisia

**Yarrow**  *Achillea*  species  Asteraceae or Compositae

*At a glance*
Number of species: Approximately 80.
Origin: Europe.
Hardiness: Often very hardy.
Habit: Mainly clump-forming herbs.
Growth rate: Fast.

*Culture*
Most soils.
Full or filtered sunlight.
Propagate by seed or division.

*Herb species*
Milfoil or Common yarrow  *Achillea Millefolium*
An attractive plant with finely divided fern-like leaves, growing to 0.5 m tall in temperate climates. Yarrow can become invasive and is considered drought tolerant and disease resistant. Yarrow was used by the American Indians for a wide range of medicinal purposes. Today its main uses are as an ornamental flower; a dried flower in potpourri and indoor flower arrangements; a dye plant; and a companion plant to lure wasps and ladybirds from other plants.

*Achillea herba-rota*
Tuft-forming plant to 20 cm tall with white flowers and attractive strong-scented foliage.

*Woolly yarrow*  *Achillea tomentosa*
Mat-forming plant to 30 cm tall with woolly foliage and yellow flowers. The flowers can be dried for potpourri or flower arrangements.

# 7 Herbs to Know and Grow

| Herb | Height | Foliage | Flower | Culture | Uses | Propagation |
|------|--------|---------|--------|---------|------|-------------|
| Aconite (*Aconitium Napellus*) | to 1 m | Dark green | Violet, blue or white | Full or part sun; moist, rich soil | Toxic medicine; cut flower | Seed or division |
| Agrimony (*Agrimonia Eupatoria*) | to 1.5 m | Hairy, rich green | Small yellow flowers | Most soils; prefers some shade; don't water leaves | Yellow dye; soothing bath; skin lotion | Seed |
| *Aloe vera* | to 80 cm | Thick fleshy | Yellow or red | Well-drained soil; drought resistant | Juice from leaves heals wounds or sores | Division |
| Angelica (*Angelica Archangelica*) | 1.5–3 m | Light green | Small white umbrella-shaped heads | Well-drained, moist, acid soil; sun or light shade | Culinary, dye and cosmetic. Soft stems and leaf petioles can be candied | Seed |
| Anise (*Pimpinella Anisum*) | 70 cm | Divided, green | Massed heads of tiny yellow to white flowers | Poor, sandy or well-drained soil | Culinary (licorice flavour); medicinal and aromatic | Seed sown direct (don't transplant) |
| Anise hyssop (*Agastache Foeniculum*) | 70–90 cm | Sweet scented | Large numbers of mauve flowers | Sunny, open spot; average soil; hardy, short-lived | Culinary— strong licorice taste; potpourri (flowers); attracts bees | Seed |
| Arnica (*Arnica montana*) | 30–70 cm | Light green | Orange to yellow | Dry organic soil; full sun | Medicinal | seed, cuttings or division |

| Herb | Height | Foliage | Flower | Culture | Uses | Propagation |
|------|--------|---------|--------|---------|------|-------------|
| Barberry (*Berberis vulgaris*) | to 2.5 m | Green, prickly | Bright yellow | Most fertile, well-drained soils; sun or part shade | Roots for yellow dye; fruit are edible | Cuttings |
| Basil, common (*Ocimum Basilicum*) | 20–60 cm | Various colours | White or purple | Well-drained, moist fertile soil; full sun | Cooking; medicinal tea | Seed |
| Basil, sacred (*Ocimum sanctum*) | 50–80 cm | Green or blue green | Pink or purple | Fertile, well-drained soil | Cosmetic; ornamental (not culinary) | Seed |
| Bay (*Laurus nobilis*) | 10–20 m | Shiny, dark green, hard | Inconspicuous | Well-drained soil; full or part sun | Culinary; cosmetic | Cuttings |
| Bayberry (*Myrtica cerifera*) | to 12 m | Dark green | Tiny and yellow | Moist, organic acid soil; full sun | Soaps; cosmetic lotions | Fresh seed |
| Bee balm (*Monarda didyma*) | 1 m | Green, soft | Brilliant pink or red heads | Fertile, organic soil; sun or shade | Culinary; cosmetic; ornamental | Seed |
| Betony (*Stachys officinalis*) | 10 cm | Grey, woolly | Mauve-red on spikes | Most soils; full or part sun | Medicinal; tea; ornamental | Seed, cuttings or division |
| Birch (*Betula papyrifera*) | 10 m | Green | Catkins | Most acid soils; part or full sun | Medicinal; culinary (drinks) | Stratified seed and grafting |
| Bloodroot (*Sanguinaria canadensis*) | 10–30 cm | Yellow-green | White, 2–4 cm diam. | Moist, organic soil; full or part sun | Medicinal; orange dye | Division |
| Boneset (*Eupatorium perfoliatum*) | 1–2 m | Long dark green leaves | White to blue | Most fertile, moist soils; full sun | Medicinal and ornamental | Cuttings |
| Borage (*Borago officinalis*) | 50–90 cm | Grey-green | Blue, star-shaped | Most soils, best sandy and fertile; full sun | Culinary (leaves stems and flowers); attracts bees | Seed |
| Boronia, brown (*Boronia megastigma*) | to 1.5 m | Green divided leaves | Brown or yellow, strongly scented | Moist, well-drained soils; prune hard after flowering; sun or part shade | Scented oil | Cuttings |
| Boronia, red (*Boronia heterophylla*) | to 1.5 m | Light green | Bright red, heavily scented | Moist drained soils, prune annually; full or part sun | Scented oil, Potpourri (flowers) | Cuttings |
| Broom (*Cytisus* spp.) | 1–2 m | Green | Yellow pea flowers | Most dry soils; full sun | Flowers for yellow dye | Cuttings or seed |

| Herb | Height | Foliage | Flower | Culture | Uses | Propagation |
|------|--------|---------|--------|---------|------|-------------|
| Burdock (*Arctium Lappa*) | 30–180 cm | White | Red to purple | Very adaptable in well-drained soils; full sun preferred | Medicinal; culinary (edible roots) | Seed |
| Calendula (*Calendula officinalis*) | 30 cm | Light green | Yellow or orange | Temperate climates; most soils; full or filtered sunlight | Medicinal; dye; culinary (flowers); cosmetic; cut flower | Seed |
| Caraway (*Carum Carvi*) | 50 cm | Finely divided, feather-like | Umbrella-shaped white heads | Sun or light shade; dry soil | Medicinal (seed); culinary (all parts) | Seed or cuttings |
| Cardamom (*Elettaria Cardamomum*) | 2–3 m | Large dark green leaves | White, blue and yellow in long racemes | Tropical climate; moist soil; shaded position | Medicinal and culinary | Cuttings |
| Castor oil plant (*Ricinus communis*) | 2–3 m | Large palm-like, green to red | Red to green flower spikes | Adaptable, most soils; full sun is best | Seeds are poisonous; seed oil used in soaps, paints, varnishes; Ornamental | Seed |
| Catnip (*Nepeta Cataria*) | 30–80 cm | Grey-green | Masses of white tubular pink spotted flowers | Light, well-drained soil; full or part sun | Medicinal; culinary; cat toys | Cuttings |
| Cayenne (*Capsicum annuum*) | to 30 cm | Bright green | Off white | Well-drained, fertile soil; full or filtered sunlight | Medicinal; culinary | Seed |
| Celandine, greater (*Chelidonium majus*) | 80 cm | Dark green, divided | Yellow, 2 cm diam. | Avoid excess water; prefers full sun; will self-seed | Dye plant | Seed |
| Chamomile, German (*Matricaria recutita*) | to 90 cm | Fern-like, green | Daisy-like, rich yellow centre and off white petals | Constantly moist, well-drained clay soil; full or part sun | Culinary (tea); hair rinse; medicinal | Seed |
| Chamomile, Roman (*Chamaemelum nobile*) | to 10 cm | Finely divided, feather-like, light green | Daisy-like, more fragrant than German chamomile | Well-drained, moist to dry sandy soil; sun or part shade | Herb lawn; culinary; medicinal | Division or seed |

| Herb | Height | Foliage | Flower | Culture | Uses | Propagation |
|---|---|---|---|---|---|---|
| Chervil (*Anthriscus Cerefolium*) | to 60 cm | Divided, light green leaves | White umbrella-like heads | Moist organic soil; filtered sun | Medicinal; culinary; pot-pourri. Leaves used like parsley | Seed |
| Chicory (*Cichorium intybus*) | to 1 m | Higher leaves sparser | Blue, daisy-like | Average but deep well-drained soil; full sun | Medicinal; culinary (leaves in salads, roots as coffee substitute) | Seed |
| Chives, common (*Allium Schoenoprasum*) | 20–40 cm | Blue-green, round stems | 1 cm diam. balls of mauve flowers | Fertile, well-drained soil; full or filtered sun | Culinary; medicinal; companion plant; dried flower | Seed or division |
| Chives, garlic (*Allium tuberosum*) | 50 cm | Flat stems | White with green markings | Rich, well-drained soil; divide annually; good light | Culinary | Division, occasionally seed |
| Cinnamon (*Cinnamomum zeylanicum*) | to 14 m | Green, young foliage red | Tiny and yellow | Warm climate; fertile, well-drained soil | Culinary; pot-pourri (bark) | Seed or cuttings |
| Clary sage (*Salvia Sclarea*) | 70–140 cm | Dull green and hairy | Purple or white | Most well-drained dry soils; full sun preferred | Culinary; to scent cosmetics; medicinal | Seed |
| Cloves (*Syzygium aromaticum*) | 5–10 m | Glossy green, sometimes hairy | White, pink or red | Warm wet humid area; most soils; sun or part shade | Medicinal; culinary; moth repellant | Seed or cuttings |
| Coffee (*Coffea arabica*) | 5–12 m | Bright green | Fragrant like jasmine | Warm climate; moist well-drained soil; full or filtered sun | Culinary and medicinal | Seed |
| *Coleus caninus* | 10–20 cm | Blue-green, fragrant | Blue-mauve on short spikes | Frost tender; most soils; full or part sun | Dog and cat repellant | Cuttings |
| Coltsfoot (*Tussilago Farfara*) | 5–10 cm | Woolly surface | 2 cm across, yellow, daisy-like | Most moist soils; prefers full sun; can be invasive | Medicinal (can be toxic); foliage sometimes used as a vegetable | Division, seed, root cuttings |

| Herb | Height | Foliage | Flower | Culture | Uses | Propagation |
|---|---|---|---|---|---|---|
| Comfrey (*Symphytum officinale*) | 50–150 cm | Woolly, green | Blue, yellow or whitish on upright spikes | Most soils but best moist and fertile; sun or shade | Medicinal; dye; cosmetic | Seed, division |
| Coriander (*Coriandrum sativum*) | 60 cm | Like parsley | White, pink, mauve or red umbrella-shaped heads | Fertile, loose, well-drained soil; full or part sun | Medicinal; culinary; potpourri | Seed |
| Corn salad (*Valerianella officinalis*) | to 20 cm | Edible salad leaves, sharp taste | White or blue | Average soil; prune after flowering; can become a weed | Culinary (younger foliage) | Seed or division |
| Costmary (*Chrysanthemum Balsamita*) | to 1 m | Grey green to white | 1 cm diam., yellow daisies | Rich, well-drained, dry loam; full or part sun | Culinary (leaves); cosmetic; ornamental | Division |
| Cumin (*Cuminum Cyminum*) | to 20 cm | Finely divided | Small heads of tiny white or rose flowers | Fertile, well-drained soil; moisture and heat; mulch | Culinary (seed as a spice, leaves with salad or vegetables) | Seed |
| Curry plant (*Helichrysum angustifolium*) | to 80 cm | Feathery, hairy, grey foliage | Small yellow flowers in 5 cm diam. clusters | Good drainage; full sun; heavy pruning at harvest | Culinary (garnish); dried flowers | Cuttings |
| Dandelion (*Taraxacum officinale*) | 10–30 cm | Green low clump | 2–3 cm diam. yellow flowers on erect stalks | Most soils; full or part sun; can become a weed | Culinary (coffee substitute, leaves can be used as greens) | Seed |
| Dill (*Anethum graveolens*) | to 90 cm | Blue-green fine feathery leaves | Yellow heads to 10 cm or more diam. | Control weeds; well-drained soil; full sun | Cosmetic oil; culinary; medicinal tea | Seed |
| Dock (*Rumex* spp.) | 30–90 cm | Light green, larger leaves close to ground | Large clusters of red or yellowish flowers on tall spikes | Loose drained soil; can be invasive | Medicinal tea eliminates toxins | Seed |
| Elderberry (*Sambucus nigra*) | to 6 m | Leaves green or variegated and deciduous | Heads of small white scented flowers to 20 cm diam. | Moist fertile soil; cool areas; sun or part shade | Dye (leaves/berries); culinary (berries); cosmetic (flowers) | Cuttings |

| Herb | Height | Foliage | Flower | Culture | Uses | Propagation |
|---|---|---|---|---|---|---|
| Elecampane (*Inula Helenium*) | 1–2 m | Bristly, lower leaves much larger | Yellow, daisy-like, to 10 cm diam. | Moist organic or clay soil; shade | Medicinal; dried flowers; culinary (in confectionary) | Root cuttings |
| Epazote (*Chenopodium ambrosioides*) | 1–1.5 m | Green to bronze-green | Inconspicuous | Most climates and soils; full sun; invasive | Culinary (Mexican food); medicinal oil | Seed |
| Eucalyptus, Blue Gum (*Eucalyptus globulus*) | to 30 m | Young growth blue, older green | Cream | Most soils; sun or part shade; harvest to 1 m above ground frequently | Medicinal; cosmetic; potpourri | Seed |
| Evening primrose (*Oenothera biennis*) | 1–2 m | Green, larger lower leaves | Masses large yellow flowers on tall spikes | Most soils; sun or part shade; invasive | Cosmetic; medicinal | Seed |
| Eyebright (*Euphrasia officinalis*) | 4–10 cm | Leafy upright stems | White or purple with yellow spots or stripes | Poor soil; grow alongside grass; full sun | Medicinal | Suckers |
| Fennel (*Foeniculum vulgare*) | 1–2 m | Feathery green or purple, aniseed scent | 8–15 cm diam. heads of tiny yellow flowers | Most well drained soils; sun or part shade; invasive | Medicinal; dye; culinary; repels fleas | Seed |
| Fenugreek (*Trigonella Foenum-graecum*) | 50–80 cm | Clover-like | White yellow or pink pea flowers | Fertile, cultivated soil; full sun | Medicinal; dye; culinary (nut flavour) | Seed |
| Feverfew (*Chrysanthemum Parthenium*) | 30–60 cm | Green to golden green | White daisy flowers with yellow centre | Most well-drained soils; full or part sun | Medicinal (eat leaves for arthritis) | Seed or cuttings |
| Five-seasons herb (*Coleus amboinicus*) | 20–40 cm | Green to blue green or with yellow margin | Blue | Prefers sandy to organic soil; full sun; warm or hot climates | Culinary (to give a savoury flavour) | Cuttings |
| Flax (*Linum usitatissimum*) | | | | Well-drained soil; full or part sun; minimal feeding; remove weeds | Fibre plant; linseed oil | Seed |
| Foxglove (*Digitalis purpurea*) | 1–1.5 m | Green and hairy | Purple, pink or white spikes | Most moist soils; sun or some shade | Medicinal; poison; ornamental | Seed |

| Herb | Height | Foliage | Flower | Culture | Uses | Propagation |
|------|--------|---------|--------|---------|------|-------------|
| Garlic (*Allium sativum*) | to 60 cm | Green to blue green | White to pinkish | Most fertile soils; good drainage; sun or partial shade | Culinary; medicinal; companion plant | Division |
| Gentian (*Gentiana lutea*) | 1–1.8 m | Pale to bright green | Large, bright yellow | Moist, well-drained, organic soil; cool climate; sun or part shade | Medicinal; ornamental | Seed (needs cold to germinate) |
| Germander (*Teucrium Chamaedrys*) | 1 m | Light green | Purple to white | Well-drained moist soil; full or part sun | Medicinal; leaves as a room freshener | Cuttings, layering or division |
| Ginger (*Zingiber officinale*) | 30–50 cm | Green | Yellow green with purple lip | Moist, well-drained, rich soil; part shade; mulch; warm areas | Medicinal (for upset stomach); culinary | Division |
| Ginseng (*Panax quinquefolius*) | 30–60 cm | Green, toothed | Pale green | Rich, well-drained acid compost; shade; hard to grow | Medicinal | Seed |
| Goldenrod (*Solidago odora*) | 1 m | Leaves smooth centres, rough edges | Rich golden yellow | Poor to average soil; well-drained; full sun | Dye; medicinal; dried flowers | Seed |
| Goldenseal (*Hydrastis canadensis*) | 15–25 cm | Dark green | Green to white | Moist organic soil; some shade; grow 5 years before harvesting roots | Medicinal; dye (yellow) | Division |
| Hawthorn (*Crataegus laevigata*) | to 5 m | Green, lobed | White, cream or pink | Fast growing; moist soils; tolerates poor and dry soils | Berries (jelly); flowers (in milk or puddings) | Cuttings |
| Herb Robert (*Geranium Robertianum*) | 30–40 cm | Reddish green | Pink | Very hardy; most soils; self-seeds | Eyewash; gargle | Seed |
| Honeysuckle (*Lonicera japonica*) | Vigorous climber | Green spotted with yellow | Cream | Invasive; moist or wet soils; sun or shade | Potpourri; medicinal | Cuttings layers |

| Herb | Height | Foliage | Flower | Culture | Uses | Propagation |
|---|---|---|---|---|---|---|
| Hop (*Humulus Lupulus*) | Climber to 10 m | Green, similar to grape leaves | Greenish white | Deep, well-drained organic soil; full sun, cool climate | Sleep pillows; antiseptic; making beer | Cuttings or suckers |
| Horehound (*Marrubium vulgare*) | 50–90 cm | Soft, green, hairy | White | Dry, well-drained loose soil; full sun | Attracts bees; culinary (tea); confectionary | Seed |
| Horseradish (*Armoracia rusticana*) | 50–80 cm | Green, to 30 cm long, wavy margin | Tiny, white | Moist, organic soil; some direct sun | Medicinal; culinary; herb bath | Root cuttings |
| Horsetail (*Equisetum* spp.) | to 40 cm | Two types: needle-like or leaf sheaths on bamboo-like stem | Spike on top of a stem | Wet organic soil; sun or some shade | Yellow dye; dried as scouring pad | Division |
| Hyssop (*Hyssopus officinalis*) | 30–80 cm | Green, fine narrow leaves | Purple to blue | Loose, well-drained soil; full or part sun | Culinary (leaves, seed and flowers); potpourri; attracts bees | Cuttings, division |
| Juniper (*Juniperus communis*) | 20 cm–12 m | Variable | Berry-like cones | Constantly moist, cool, mulched soil; cool to mild area | Medicinal; berries used in gin | Cuttings |
| Lady's Mantle (*Alchemilla vulgaris*) | 30–50 cm | Roughly rounded to 15 cm diam. | Greenish-yellow | Part shade; moist soil | Dried flowers | Division |
| Lamb's Ears (*Stachys byzantina*) | creeping | Grey hairy fragrant leaves | Purple or pink upright spikes | Most soils; prefers full sun; responds to feeding | Dried foliage in wreaths or posies; tea from fresh leaves | Division |
| Lavender, English (*Lavandula angustifolia*) | to 1.2 m | Blue-grey | Mauve | Most well-drained soils; some direct sunlight preferred | Potpourri; cosmetics; culinary | Cuttings |
| Lavender, French (*Lavandula dentata*) | to 1 m | Grey | Mauve | Most well-drained soils; full or part sun | Potpourri; dried flowers; crafts | Cuttings |

| Herb | Height | Foliage | Flower | Culture | Uses | Propagation |
|------|--------|---------|--------|---------|------|-------------|
| Lavender, Italian (*Lavandula Stoechas*) | to 85 cm | Grey | Rich purple | Hardy; some drought tolerance; avoid waterlogged soil | Crafts; dried flowers | Cuttings |
| Lavender, cotton (*Santolina Chamaecyparissus*) | to 70 cm | Silver-grey | Yellow buttons | Light, drained lime soil; full or part sun | Dried flowers; dye; potpourri | Cuttings |
| Lemon balm (*Melissa officinalis*) | to 80 cm | Green, crinkled surface, lemon scented | Cream | Most soils; sun or shade; can become invasive | Culinary (leaves a lemon substitute) | Seed, division |
| Lemon verbena (*Aloysia triphylla*) | 2–5 m | Green, lemon scented | Pale mauve | Moist, fertile soil; full or part sun | Lemon substitute; digestive aid | Cuttings |
| Licorice (*Glycyrrhiza glabra*) | 1–2 m | Yellow-green, Divided | Purple or mauve, pea-like | Fertile, moist soil; good drainage; some shade | Culinary; cosmetic; medicinal | Seed or sucker cuttings |
| Lovage (*Levisticum officinale*) | 1.7 m | Glossy, dark green, celery scent | 3–10 cm diam. yellow heads | Well-drained, rich, moist soil; full or part sun | Culinary (tastes like celery) | Seed or division |
| Madder (*Rubia tinctorum*) | to 1 3 m | 5–8 cm long prickly leaves | Yellow, small | Deep well-drained soil | Dye | Division |
| Marjoram (*Origanum Majorana*) | to 35 cm | Grey-green | White or pink | Well-drained, weed-free soil; full or filtered sun | Culinary; gargle; tea; antiseptic | Cuttings |
| Marshmallow (*Althaea officinalis*) | 1.2–1.8 m | Grey-green | White to pink | Most moist or wet soils; full sun | Culinary (young leaves); medicinal | Seed, division or cuttings |
| Mint, Applemint (*Mentha suaveolens*) | 50–85 cm | Green to grey-green, furry | White or pink | Wet organic or clay soils; sun or shade; invasive | Culinary (drinks, sweets, jelly) | Division or cuttings |
| Mint, common (*Mentha arvensis*) | 60 cm | Green | Mauve or white | Any moist to wet soil; invasive | Culinary | Division |
| Mint, Peppermint (*Mentha × piperita*) | 50–90 cm | Deep green to purplish-green | Pink to purple | Moist, organic soil; mulch is beneficial; full or filtered sun | Oil; culinary; medicinal; insect and rodent repellant | Division or cuttings |

| Herb | Height | Foliage | Flower | Culture | Uses | Propagation |
|---|---|---|---|---|---|---|
| Mint, Spearmint (*Mentha spicata*) | 50–80 cm | Green, crinkled | Pink, purple or white | Moist, mulched soil; sun or shade | Confectionery | Division |
| Monkshood (*Aconitium Napellus*) | to 1 m | Divided leaves | Violet to blue | Moist, organic soil; some shade | All parts poisonous; yields aconite—used medicinally | Seed or division |
| Mugwort (*Artemisia vulgaris*) | to 1.8 m | Deeply divided, grey green | Yellowish to brownish | Well-drained soil; full sun | Moth repellant; dried foliage; herb bath | Seed |
| Mustard (*Brassica hirta*) | 1 m | Lobed or toothed | Masses of tiny yellow flowers | Rich, well-drained soil; full sun | Culinary; companion plant for cabbage | Seed |
| Myrrh (*Commiphora myrrha*) | to 3 m | Divided, 3 oval-shaped segments | Brown fruits | Very hot, dry climate | Soap; perfume; mosquito repellant | Try cuttings |
| Nasturtium (*Tropaeolum majus*) | Vigorous creeper | Circular, soft, green or variegated | Variable colours red, yellow, orange, etc | Most moist to wet soils; sun or shade | Culinary (leaves and flowers in salads); companion plant to control aphis | Seed |
| Neem (*Azadirachtia indica*) | to 20 m | Pinnate leaves | | Infertile, well-drained soils; full sun; warm frost-free areas | Insect repellant | Ripe seed |
| Onion (*Allium Cepa*) | to 60 cm | Hollow round blue-green | White ball like flower head | Moist, well-drained soils; feed well; full sun | Antiseptic; dye; dried flower; culinary | Seed |
| Oregano (*Origanum vulgare*) | 30 cm | Blue-green, strongly scented | White to purple | Most well-drained soils; full sun | Culinary; herb baths; medicinal | Cuttings |
| Orris root (*Iris × germanica* var. *florentina*) | to 1.5 m | Long sword-like blue-green leaves | White with blue | Rich, well-drained soil; full sun; divide clumps every 2 years | Fixative for scented products | Division |
| Parsley, curled (*Petroselinum crispum*) | to 30 cm | Bright green curled leaves | Small greenish yellow | Well-drained, moist organic soil; full or filtered sun | Culinary; cosmetic; source of vitamins A and C | Seed (slow to germinate) |

| Herb | Height | Foliage | Flower | Culture | Uses | Propagation |
|---|---|---|---|---|---|---|
| Pennyroyal (*Mentha Pulegium*) | Creeper to 30 cm | Oval green | Small lilac head | Moist, organic soil; filtered sun | Insect repellant; herb lawn | Division or cuttings |
| Plantain (*Plantago major*) | 15–40 cm | Long oval shape forms rossetes | Small yellow-green spikes | Very hardy, moist well-drained soil; full or part sun | Dye; young leaves eaten like spinach; chew root for toothache | Seed |
| Potentilla (*Potentilla* spp.) | to 40 cm | Variable shape, silvery beneath | Yellow, white or red | Most well-drained soils; part or full sun | Red dye; medicinal; ornamental | Division |
| Rose (*Rosa* spp.) | to 1.5 m or more | Glossy green pinnate | Variable size, colour and numbers | Well-drained organic or clay soil; full or part sun; prune annually | Culinary (fruits); potpourri (petals) | Cuttings or grafting |
| Rosemary (*Rosmarinus officinalis*) | to 1.2 m | Grey-green needle-like | Small pale blue | Any well-drained soil; avoid fresh manure; full sun | Medicinal; herb bath; cosmetic; dye; culinary | Cuttings |
| Rue (*Ruta graveolens*) | to 90 cm | Blue-green scented leaves | Yellow flower heads | Excellent drainage; good ventilation; full sun | Medicinal; companion plant | Seed or cuttings |
| Safflower (*Carthamus tinctorius*) | to 90 cm | Pointed oval leaf | Orange to yellow | Poor, dry soil; full sun | Dye; culinary (use flowers) | Seed |
| Saffron (*Crocus sativus*) | to 30 cm | Dark green, grass-like | Large white scented with yellow and red | Sandy, mulched, well-drained soil; cool climates | Dye; medicinal; culinary | Division |
| Sage, blue (*Salvia Clevelandii*) | 70 cm–1 m | Greyish-green hairy | Blue flowers | Good drainage; full or filtered sun | Culinary (leaves); potpourri | Cuttings |
| Sage, common (*Salvia officinalis*) | 50–90 cm | Silvery grey hairy | Blue, pink or white | Good drainage, loose fertile, weed-free soil; full or part sun; prune regularly | Insect repellant; medicinal; cosmetic culinary | Cuttings or seed |
| Sage, Mexican (*Salvia leucantha*) | 1–2 m | Greyish-green hairy beneath | White woolly flowers with purple | Hardy; most well-drained soils; full or part sun | Dried flowers; potpourri | Cuttings |

Goldern marjoram (*Origanum vulgare* 'Aureum')

Apple mint (*Mentha suaveolens*)

Peppermint (*Mentha × piperata*)

*Mentha* species

Rosemary (*Rosmarinus officinalis*)

Variegated nasturtium (*Tropaeolom majus*)

Parsley

Prostrate rosemary

Salad burnet (*Poterium sanguisorba*)

Lavender cotton (*Santolina chamaecyparissus*)
Pelargonium species 'Attar of Roses'

Rue (*Ruta graveolens*)

Common sage (*Salvia officinalis*)
Cinnamon geranium

Variegated scented geranium

Sorrel (*Rumex scutatus*)

Southernwood (*Artemesia abrotanum*)

Thyme (*Thymus vulgaris*)
Variegated lemon thyme (*Thymus* × *citriodorus*)

Tansy (*Tanacetum vulgare*)
*Thymus herba-barona*

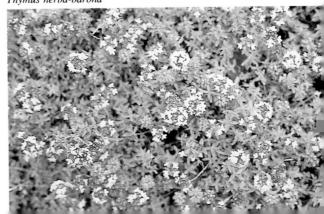

Valerian (*Valeriana officinalis*)

Vietnamese or hot mint (*Polygonum odoratum*)

Winter savory (*Satureja montana*)

*Spiraea* species

Wormwood hedge

Herb vinegar

| Herb | Height | Foliage | Flower | Culture | Uses | Propagation |
|---|---|---|---|---|---|---|
| Sage, pineapple (*Salvia elegans*) | 70–90 cm | Hairy beneath; pineapple-scented | Brilliant red | Most well-drained soils; full or part sun | Culinary (drinks, confectionery, etc.) | Cuttings or division |
| St John's Wort (*Hypericum perforatum*) | 60 cm | Small light green, oil glands | Bright yellow with black dots | Most soils; full or part sun; short-lived; can be invasive | Yellow or red dye; medicinal | Division |
| Salad burnet (*Poterium Sanguisorba*) | 30–90 cm | Toothed and rounded | Head of small pinkish flowers | Moist, well-drained soil; full or filtered sun | Culinary (leaves in salads) | Seed |
| Savory, summer (*Satureja hortensis*) | 30–45 cm | Small narrow on reddish stems | Pale pink or white | Average soil; full sun | Tea for upset stomachs; culinary | Seed (germinates fast) |
| Savory, winter (*Satureja montana*) | 20–45 cm | Narrow strongly scented | White or pink | Light, well-drained soil | Tea for stomach upsets; culinary | Seed (slow) |
| Scented geranium (*Pelargonium* spp.) | 90 cm | Velvety, fern-like, fragrant | Variable in colour, size and shape | Dryish, organic soils; full or filtered sun; prune frequently to shape | Culinary; potpourri scented oils; medicinal | Cuttings |
| Soapwort (*Saponaria officinalis*) | to 90 cm | 3-veined, non-hairy | Pink or white | Full or filtered sun; once established is hardy; most well-drained soils; often invasive | Foliage used as a soap substitute | Seed or division |
| Sorrel, garden (*Rumex Acetosa*) | to 90 cm | Green to reddish | Reddish spikes | Loose, moist soil; full sun or part shade; invasive | Culinary (leaves used as salad or cooked vegetable) | Division or seed |
| Stinging nettle (*Urtica dioica*) | 0.6–1.5 m | Dark green with bristly hairs | Minute greenish cluster | Most moist soils; sun or shade | Dye; medicinal, culinary (young tops cooked like spinach) | Seed |
| Sweet Cicely (*Myrrhis odorata*) | to 2.5 m | Fern-like | Cream to white heads | Rich, well-drained soil; best mulched; semi-shade | Potpourri; craft; culinary | Seed—needs cold period to germinate |

| Herb | Height | Foliage | Flower | Culture | Uses | Propagation |
|------|--------|---------|--------|---------|------|-------------|
| Sweet flag (*Acorus Calamus*) | 1–1.5 m | Reed or iris-like, glossy green | Yellow-green | Moist or wet organic soil; shade; control weeds | Powdered root used as cinnamon substitute | Division |
| Sweet woodruff (*Galium odoratum*) | 20–30 cm | Small, dark green | Small, white | Well-drained, moist organic soil; shade; control weeds | Flowers as a tea; potpourri; perfume | Seed |
| Tansy (*Tanacetum vulgare*) | 0.8–1.2 m | Green fern-like foliage, deciduous | Clusters of yellow buttons | Most soils; sun or part shade; mildly invasive | Fly repellant; dried flowers; dye | Division or seed |
| Tea tree (*Melaleuca alternifolia*) | to 6 m | Green stiff leaves, 2–3 cm long | White bottle-brush flowers | Most moist soils; full or part sun; prune regularly | Antiseptic oil; insect repellant | Seed or cuttings |
| Thyme, common (*Thymus vulgaris*) | 15–30 cm | Tiny oval, grey-green leaves | White or mauve | Dry, well-drained friable soil; full or filtered sun | Medicinal; antiseptic; culinary | Cuttings or division |
| Valerian (*Valeriana officinalis*) | 80 cm | Feathery | Small pink, fragrant | Fertile, moist, organic soil; full or part sun | To perfume soap; a soothing herb bath | Division |
| Vervain (*Verbena officinalis*) | to 80 cm | Dark green | Pale purple | Fertile, moist soil; part sun | Soothing herb bath | Seed |
| Violet (*Viola odorata*) | 5–10 cm | Green, round to heart-shaped | Commonly purple, also white or pink | Feed well; moist compost; prefers filtered light | Culinary (flowers); oils; crafts; perfumes | Division |
| Wintergreen (*Gaultheria procumbens*) | to 10 cm | Creeping, thick, shiny upper surface | Single white flowers, 5 mm long, nodding | Moist, loose soil; part shade | Culinary; herb baths; cosmetic; medicinal | Layers, seed, cuttings or division |
| Witch hazel (*Hamamelis virginiana*) | 3–4 m | Roughly circular, to 15 cm diam. | Bright yellow | Deep, fertile soil; plenty of room to spread; hardy | Medicinal | Seed or layering |
| Woad (*Isatis tinctoria*) | to 1.2 m | Blue green, to 10 cm long | Golden yellow | Fertile, well-drained soil; full sun | Blue dye | Seed in spring |
| Wormwood (*Artemisia Absinthium*) | 1–1.5 m | Grey divided, scented foliage | Heads of yellow button flowers | Well-drained clay or loam; full or part sun; very hardy | Repels snails and snakes; used to make vermouth | Cuttings |

| Herb | Height | Foliage | Flower | Culture | Uses | Propagation |
|---|---|---|---|---|---|---|
| Yarrow (*Achillea Millefolium*) | 30–50 cm | Fern-like | Red, pink or white | Very hardy in most soils; full or filtered sun | Dye; dried flowers; medicinal; craft; cosmetic; attracts beneficial insects | Seed or division |

# Appendixes

## Home Study Courses

The Australian Horticultural Correspondence School is a government-recognised private college. It conducts over 150 different home study courses including hobby, certificate and advanced certificate courses covering most areas of horticulture including herbs, landscaping, crops, roses and cottage gardens. Courses offered include:

Herbs: A six-lesson course for the beginner on growing and using herbs.
Herb Culture: A comprehensive 200-hour course for the enthusiast (amateur or professional) dealing with identification, culture, harvesting and processing a wide range of herbs. Approximately half of the course is devoted to a detailed study of the main varieties of herbs grown commercially.
Advanced Certificate in Applied Management (Herbs): A comprehensive course covering both management studies and herb industry studies (including herb identification, culture, harvesting, processing, making and marketing herb products, and managing a herb business).
Cottage Garden Design: Over eight lessons covering such things as cottage plants, topiary, ornaments, furniture, gazebos and planting design. In this course you will learn to prepare a proper landscape design for a cottage garden.
Roses: An eight-lesson course covering identification, pruning, propagation, pests and diseases, culture and landscaping with all types of roses (including floribundas, hybrid teas, miniatures and old varieties).
Organic Gardening: This course shows you how to grow plants in a natural way, without the use of chemicals or artificial fertilisers. Learn about crop rotation, compost making, soil building, companion planting, the proper use of organic fertilisers and other natural gardening techniques.

Other courses of interest to the herb enthusiast include Culinary Herbs, Growing Lavender, Scented Plants, Medicinal Herbs, Starting a Craft Business, Self Sufficiency, Hydroponics, Commercial Vegetable Growing and Cut Flower Growing.

Full details of these and other courses can be obtained from:
The Australian Horticultural Correspondence School
P.O. Box 2092, Nerang East, QLD 4211. Ph: (075) 304 855
or 264 Swansea Rd, Lilydale, VIC 3140. Ph: (03) 736 1882

## Further reading

The following publications are recommended by the author of this book:

*Gardening with Herbs* Garden Guide magazine series
*More Gardening with Herbs* Garden Guide magazine series
*The Herbalist* by Joseph Meyer (Meyer Books)
*The Old Herb Doctor* by Joseph Meyer (Meyer Books)
*Lavender, Sweet Lavender* by Judyth McLeod (Kangaroo Press)
*Herbs and Flowers* by Jennifer Wilkinson (Inkata Press)
*The Book of Mint* by Denise Greig (Kangaroo Press)
*Companion Plants* by Philbrick and Greig (Kangaroo Press)
*Colourful and Fragrant Gardens* Greenleaf magazine series
*101 Natural Gardening Ideas* Garden Guide magazine series
*Growing Vegetables* by Mason and Lawrence (Kangaroo Press)
*Natural Gardening* by Jeffrey Hodges (Viking O'Neil)
*Oh for An Onion* by Denise Greig (Kangaroo Press)
*Grass Roots* magazine series (Night Owl)
*Starting a Nursery or Herb Farm* by John Mason (Night Owl)

# Index